Twice-told True Tales of the Blue Ridge & Great Smokies

Mead Parce

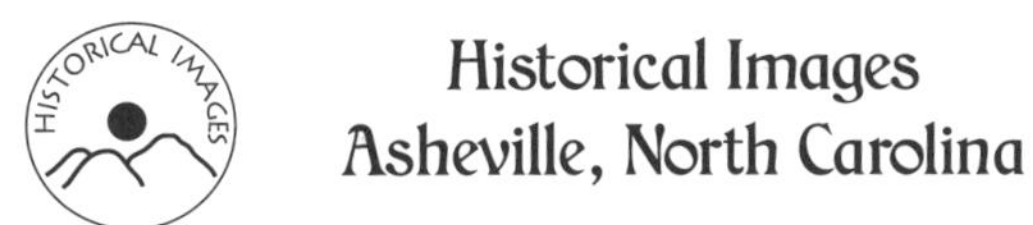

Historical Images
Asheville, North Carolina

Bright Mountain Books, Inc.
138 Springside Road
Asheville, NC 28803

Historical Images is an imprint of Bright Mountain Books, Inc.

Originally published by Harmon Den Press, 1995, under the same title. Five additional tales were written for this edition.

Printed in the United States of America

ISBN: 0-914875-37-X

Library of Congress Cataloging-in-Publication Data

Parce, Mead.
Twice-told true tales of the Blue Ridge & Great Smokies / Mead Parce.—Enlarged ed.
p. cm.
Originally published: Hendersonville, N.C. : Harmon Den Press, c1995.
With five additional stories.
Includes index.
ISBN 0-914875-37-X
1. Blue Ridge Mountains—Social life and customs—Anecdotes. 2. Great Smoky Mountains (N.C. and Tenn.)—Social life and customs—Anecdotes. I. Title: Twice-told true tales of the Blue Ridge and Great Smokies. II. Title.
F262.B6 P37 2001
975.5—dc21

00-012585

Contents

Preface

Years ago in southern highland homes, farmhouses, and cabins the fireplace hearth was the focal point of family life. The hearth warmed the home, farmhouse, and cabin and provided light and the heat with which to cook meals. When chores were done, the hearth was the backdrop for social life and entertainment—banjo and fiddle music, songs, dancing, and storytelling.

Folk music, religious harmony music, clog dancing, and storytelling survive and flourish even today in the Blue Ridge and Great Smoky Mountains of Western North Carolina and eastern Tennessee. Over the years twice-told tales have become thrice-told tales—embellished and polished by storytellers in the mountains. Some are Jack Tales whose origin in Scotland, England, and Ireland coincide with the familiar folktale, "Jack and the Beanstalk." Others are true tales of history.

Eleven of the following stories are historical; the others are folktales told as history. Each involves Western North Carolina. Because the stories are historical, they are basically twice-told tales. The stories are written to provide some historical perspective on the people and culture of the southern highlands.

For example, one of the major influences in the cultural, economic, and social development of Asheville is George Vanderbilt's "House on a Hill—Biltmore." The story of how Vanderbilt inherited his money as well as his love of the arts is told in the Biltmore chapter. One of the stereotypes of the mountains is the moonshiner. The story of illegal liquor, called "blockade," is told in "Blockade and Blockaders." How a logging railroad penetrated the Western North Carolina wilderness is told in the chapter titled "Western North Carolina's Mile-High Railroad." There is a chapter on Thomas Wolfe, Asheville's most famous citizen. The story about being one's own grandfather and grandmother, while true in history, is now folklore, along with the "Tale of Abraham Lincoln's Birth." The stories about "The Mountain Lily," "The White Chief Who Saved the Cherokees" and the "First Automobile Trips Over the Smokies" are historical.

Where these stories were once told in front of a roaring fire on a cold winter's night in cabins and homes set amid the coves, hollows, and villages, today they are part of the written lore. The stories are both tales and trails to be explored.

Acknowledgments

No author or writer is alone in his work. Whether via encouragement, inspiration, research, guidance, friendship, technical knowledge, counsel, editing, or production, there is a legion of people and institutions to whom an author or writer is deeply indebted. I am indebted to many people in producing this book for the enjoyment of readers interested in the Blue Ridge and the Smokies.

The story, "A Festive Hangin" could not have been done without the help of Mrs. Edna Justus of Edneyville, North Carolina, neither could have the story of Biltmore House without the cooperation and friendship of George Vanderbilt's grandson, William A. V. Cecil and his gracious wife, Mimi. Frank L. FitzSimons, Sr., and his son, Frank L. Jr., offered any stories and information I might need from Frank Sr.'s fine trilogy, *Along the Banks of the Oklawaha*.

Attorney James H. Toms of Hendersonville furnished much of the material on Thomas Wolfe. Sadie Smathers Patton, author of a history on Henderson County, also furnished first-person accounts of Wolfe and his family. The story on moonshining couldn't have been written without James Bartlett of Mills River, a longtime Alcoholic Beverage Control officer in Henderson County.

Penelope Niven, author of *Carl Sandburg, A Biography*, and Robert Morgan, poet-author and professor of English at Cornell University, are writers whose stories of the Blue Ridge provide valuable insight into the culture of the mountains. Lucius Ingle of Asheville provided first person accounts of the mile-high railroad to Mount Mitchell from Black Mountain.

Others I would like to thank include Clarence Goode and Buddy Chapman, colleagues at the *Times-News*; Alice Lawson for her editing; Emily Keeling, Nancy Snowden, Zoda Mae Hawkins, Eleanor Healy, Joyce Fogarty, Pat Bendl, and Carolyn Vaughn of the Henderson County Public Library for their research help; personnel at the State Library in Raleigh, the Pack Library in Asheville, and the Ramsey Library at the University of North Carolina at Asheville; Jimmie Fain, my predecessor as editor of the *Times-News*; Sandra Hayes, director of printing for the University of North Carolina at Asheville, and Diane Boone of the UNCA Printing Services office; Karen Gibbs, manager of the Eastern National Park and Monument Association bookstore at the Carl Sandburg Home at Flat Rock, North Carolina, and Carolyn Sierk, who for many years owned Carolyn's Book Shoppe, Hendersonville, North Carolina.

And, of course, my special debt to Diane Darden Parce, my wife, for her patience and forbearance over the years in traveling the back roads of the Blue Ridge and Smokies to search out a people and their heritage.

My sincere apologies to anyone I have carelessly omitted.

Twice-told True Tales of the Blue Ridge & Great Smokies

Western North Carolina's Mile-high Passenger Railroad

Western North Carolina once had a mile-high passenger railroad that crossed the Blue Ridge Parkway at the 354.6 mile mark and ran to a special camp just below the summit of Mount Mitchell. It came about when the timber company of Perley and Crockett decided to add passenger cars to its logging railroad operated from the village of Black Mountain east of Asheville along 21 miles of track through the timberlands in the Black Mountains to the 5,800-foot contour line on Mount Mitchell.

The story actually began in 1911 when two lumbermen, C. A. Dickey and J. C. Campbell acquired timber rights to nine thousand acres on the southern and eastern flanks of the Black Mountains and Mount Mitchell. The old way of hauling timber out of the mountains was by horse team or oxen. Sawyers would cut the huge trees on the slopes, then remove them by either dragging the logs along a logging trail or by way of a "ball hoot," the practice of felling a tree at the top of a ridge or lower, and sending it to the bottom on its own in a crashing slide that took out everything in its path. This got the logs to the bottom of the hollow where they could be dragged out and loaded on wagons for shipment to a mill. If the logs were dragged by oxen or horse team along the trails, there was less damage to other trees. However, if logs were ball hooted down the steep sides of the hollows, they would crash and trash every bit of undergrowth, trees, and saplings they came near on their way down. In later years cable skidders were used to lower logs to the trails in place of the destructive ball hoot method. All of this was a slow and difficult process. The loggers and teams would struggle to get just one huge log out of the steep-sloped woods. For this reason, timber cutting remained a local enterprise until the early 1900s.

The change came when timber men from Maine, upstate New York, Pennsylvania, and Michigan eyed the Southern Appalachians after they had exhausted the supply of saw logs in their states through clear cutting of every available tract. When the northern timber men came, they brought with them a concept folks in the mountains never thought of—railroads, logging railroads to be precise.

When the idea of a railroad to the top of the mountains in the Blue Ridge and Great Smokies came up, many old-timers laughed. The roadbeds would be too steep, the effort too costly, and engineering too great, they said. It had taken millions of dollars, convict labor, and many years to bring the Western North Carolina Railroad from Old Fort to Asheville and many more millions and years to run the tracks up the Blue Ridge from Spartanburg, South Carolina, through Saluda Gap to Hendersonville and Asheville. People asked how could a timber company propose to build a twenty-one-mile narrow-gauge line into the steepest part of the Black Mountains and still make money? There were plenty of skeptics.

If C. A. Dickey and J. C. Campbell heard the snickers, they simply ignored them. The railroad to haul their timber was built on a 5½ percent grade—very low for a logging railroad—over an eighteen-mile distance in a little more than a year. That feat alone dampened any laughter. The climb, it should be noted, was forty-five hundred feet to the top from a starting point near the village of Black Mountain. Later the roadbed would be extended to fifty-eight thousand feet above sea level, hence a mile-high railroad. Another remarkable item in the construction of the railroad is there were no curves in the roadbed. Instead, the builders used nine switchbacks and three trestles. The switchbacks climbed the mountains like herringbone tracks left by skiers climbing a hillside.

Lucius Ingle of Asheville, an employee of Southern Railway from 1924 until his retirement in 1948, remembers working on the logging railroad in 1919 as a sixteen year old:

> We'd put six cars ahead of a Climax engine and six cars behind to go up the mountain. The engine would climb as high as it could on the grade before switching to a gentler grade that would continue to rise. This switching back and forth up the mountain enabled the train to go up the mountain without any curves in the track. The Climax engine also was gear driven, thus providing more pulling power than conventional road steam engines.

Ingle lived just north of Asheville as a young person. In the summer of 1919, he and a group of young men would catch Southern Railway's Number 12 train out of Knoxville, Tennessee, to Asheville at the Craggy flag stop. They would then ride to Asheville, and thence to Black Mountain, where on Sunday afternoon the logging train would take them to Camp Alice right below the summit of Mount Mitchell. They would work on the railroad during the week, replacing ties and maintaining the one track logging line. "On Friday night we'd ride the logging train down the mountain to Black Mountain. There we'd catch the train from Statesville to Asheville. Then we'd take the next Knoxville-bound train, and get off at Craggy flag stop. Occasionally I'd have to work as a sixteen-year-old brakeman on the logging trains," he said. "Five of us would have to set the hand brakes. Those trains didn't have air brakes as they do today."

Until the railroad penetrated the wilderness on the flanks of Mount Mitchell, the only way to reach the summit was a long hike along trails either from the Yancey County side of the mountain or from Black Mountain. The trips were often several days, although some hikers could make the twenty one-mile trip to the top in one day, and stay overnight on the mountain before returning the following day. Travel was rugged for mountaineers. Even the horses often used to pack into the wilderness found the going rough. Only the bear hunters who made a religion of the annual hunt enjoyed the trails. Few people made the trip before the logging railroad, but those who did exclaimed about the view to be seen from the top of the mountain, once called Black Dome.

In 1913, Dickey and Campbell sold the timber rights to two Williamsport, Pennsylvania, lumbermen, Allen P. Perley and his son-in-law, W. H. Crockett. Both the price of timber, which had fallen drastically because of competition, and the cost of pushing the railroad higher up the mountain to obtain more spruce caused Dickey and Campbell to sell.

Perley and Crockett was a lumber company that was nearly wiped out in June 1889, when a massive flood struck the Susquehanna River at Williamsport. At the time, Williamsport was known as the lumber capital of the world because of the number of sawmills along the banks of the river. It was during this period that Maine lumbermen such as Allen Perley, father of Fred A. Perley—who would run the Black Mountain operation after Dickey and Campbell, logged upstate New York and Pennsylvania. When Perley and Crockett finished logging the West Branch Valley near Williamsport, they moved operations to West Virginia and Virginia. They eyed Western North Carolina when they heard Dickey and Campbell wanted to sell.

Dickey and Campbell's cash flow problems set the stage for the arrival of Perley and Crockett and Allen Perley's son, Fred A. Perley, at Black Mountain. Fred Perley became a business leader in Black Mountain and Western North Carolina, and his impact is still apparent today.

Back then there was a need for spruce in the fledgling aviation industry just developing in the United States and France. Early manufacturers of aircraft such as the Wright Brothers of Dayton, Ohio, and Glenn Curtis, the Hammondsport, New York, inventor and aircraft builder, used spruce for spars in the airframe and wings of their aircraft. The spars, of course, were covered with linen cloth which was stretched by painting it with lacquer.

To obtain spruce and balsam, Perley and Crockett pushed their recently acquired railroad even higher in the mountain range to just below the stands of spruce and balsam, so the logs, once cut, could be loaded on flat cars for the run to the mill at Black Mountain with little effort. Records of the time indicate the logs were dumped off flat cars into a pond at Black Mountain and then rafted to the band mill located between Black Mountain and Ridgecrest. Trees under eight inches in diameter went to the paper plant of Champion Paper and Fiber Company at Canton, North Carolina, west of Asheville on the Pigeon River. The larger size trees went to the mill for spars and other wood building products.

When people found out the railroad came within a mile of the summit of Mount Mitchell, they asked Perley and Crockett's managers if they could ride the logging trains. A few such trips were organized for special groups. These were successful, and the firm's managers gave some thought to organizing additional tours. The owners saw the potential of a new revenue source, so they authorized construction of some rough wooden coaches to run behind the three forty-two-ton Climax and two thirty-six-ton Shay engines used by the loggers.

Passengers didn't care how rough the coaches; they wanted to see the world from the top of Mount Mitchell, a place they'd heard about all their lives but had never seen because of the difficulty of getting there and back on foot. The first passengers were carried in 1913. The increased traffic didn't interfere with logging, so Perley and Crockett decided to promote the trips. They hired a man named Col. Sanford H. Cohen to serve as general passenger agent for the railroad.

Colonel Cohen formerly managed the Greater Western North Carolina Association, a tourist bureau organized to promote tourism in Western North Carolina after businessmen in Asheville and environs found out people would pay good money to stay in hotels, rooming houses, and camps to escape the summer heat of the low country of South Carolina, Georgia, and Florida and admire the beauty of the mountains in the process. Colonel Cohen knew all about searing heat as well as making a dollar on tourism. He developed the Isle of Palms located outside of Charleston, South Carolina, before finding his way to the mountains as did thousands of Charlestonians before him. It should be noted that Flat Rock, located a few miles or so south of Hendersonville, has been known as "Little Charleston in the Mountains" since the 1850s when wealthy planters and businessman built summer cottages on large estates to flee malaria and the heat.

Colonel Cohen also was one of the early masters of public relations hyperbole in an era when the mountain people around Asheville were modest about the natural beauty they took for granted. One of the colonel's advertisements in the *Asheville Citizen* read:

The World's Greatest Scenic Mountain Trip

Mount Mitchell—Altitude 6,711 feet

The Top of Eastern America

Over the Mount Mitchell Railroad, the Scenic Marvel, the Road of Mountain Magnificence, Going to the Crest of the Land of the Sky, Above the Clouds, The Trip Presents a Perfect Panorama of Unsurpassed Magnificence, Grandeur, Beauty and Sublimity, Unequaled on the Globe.

What Colonel Cohen didn't say is that passengers on the mile-high railroad to the summit of Mount Mitchell would also see the utter devastation caused by the logging operations of the railroad's owners, Messrs. Perley and Crockett, as well as the previous owners, Dickey and Campbell. Much of the nine-thousand-acre timber tract had been clear cut; the mountains were bald except for stumps and slash left to burn.

Despite the problem of denuded slopes, the passenger rail service was a huge success. Thousands of people paid to ride the train up the mountain in the morning to Camp Alice, location of a dining-hall-style restaurant, tent sites, and dormitories. From there they could hike to the summit of Mount Mitchell, then return in the afternoon to Black Mountain in time to catch a Southern Railway passenger train back to Asheville. It was a grand one-day trip for an outing.

The mile-high railroad lasted only four years. In 1919, with the recent end of the Great War to End All Wars, known to us as World War I, the Perley and Crockett company announced it was suspending traffic on the railroad so it could remove the rest of the timber on the tract. The announcement set off a firestorm of protest by the Asheville Board of Trade because tourism in the mountains was rapidly becoming the number-one industry, and the railroad was a drawing card. But the timber barons held fast; passenger service would end and it did.

By 1921, Perley and Crockett ended timber operations on the nine thousand acres that by now looked like a war zone with hardly a sapling growing. Earlier the clear cutting of the mountain provoked a major protest led by North Carolina Gov. Locke Craig, who once hunted bear and deer in the coves and along the ridges of the Black Mountains. He led the fight to save the crown of Mount Mitchell—now a state park—in 1915 before Perley and Crockett's loggers reached that point. In the 1970s, an unsuccessful fight was waged by Western North Carolina's two daily newspapers, the *Asheville Citizen-Times* and the Hendersonville *Times-News*, to make Mount Mitchell State Park part of Pisgah National Forest. The idea was rejected by the U.S. Forest Service.

Fred Perley and C. A. Dickey, two of the four timber men involved in the ownership and logging of the mountain, also headed the Mount Mitchell Development Company. Perley couldn't forget the thousands of people a year who went up the mountain for the four years the railroad was in operation. He and Dickey proposed a motor road to the summit. When the tracks and ties came up at the end of timber operations, the two men had the grade of the railroad aligned in places and resurfaced with cinders. Colonel Cohen returned to the firm, and this time coined the phrase: "Making the Apex of Appalachia Accessible." The motor road became as popular as the railroad had been. People flocked to the mountain by riding Ford Model-T cars to Camp Alice. The promoters expanded Camp Alice, so visitors could stay overnight and hike trails near the summit.

The motor road continued to be a toll road for access to the mountain through the 1920s and mid-1930s. Historians note that traffic was one-way, up in the morning and down in the afternoon. Mount Washington in New Hampshire continues to have a two-way toll road to the summit similar to the Mount Mitchell road. Pike's Peak in Colorado has a two-way, nontoll road to the summit. There are others. In the 1930s, the route of the long sought Blue Ridge Parkway was approved, and work began on a section from public roads over the ridge north of Mount Mitchell to the present entrance of Mount Mitchell State Park. Once public roads were linked to the mountain, the toll roads (another private toll road went to Mount Mitchell from Burnsville) passed into history.

Today there is easy access to Mount Mitchell via the Blue Ridge Parkway, but from 1915 until 1919, the mile-high passenger railroad provided high adventure to those seeking the thrill of reaching the summit of eastern America's highest mountain peak.

NOTE: Camp Alice became part of a Civilian Conservation Corps camp in the 1930s. The buildings were torn down many years ago, and replaced by a series of Adirondack-style shelters for use by hikers, horse trail riders, and other groups for overnight stays. Visitors interested in visiting the old Camp Alice site may reach the place by parking at the ranger station near the entrance to Mount Mitchell State Park, and walking about a mile or so along the old roadbed of the railroad, now a one-lane road, to the open spot where the shelters are located. A rocky trail leads from old Camp Alice to the summit of Mount Mitchell. However, the main road to Mount Mitchell is the way most visitors now visit the mountain and memorial to Dr. Elisha Mitchell, explorer of the Black Mountains.

You Can Go Home Again—Sometimes

Thomas Wolfe is now honored and revered by Asheville residents, but it wasn't always that way. In fact, Wolfe once wrote a book called *You Can't Go Home Again.* The Asheville author found that a prophet is without honor in his hometown if he writes fictional characterizations based on people he has known. Therein lies a tale.

It began in October 1929, when the New York firm of Charles Scribner's Sons published Wolfe's first novel. *Look Homeward, Angel.* A graduate of the University of North Carolina at Chapel Hill with a B.A. degree in English, Wolfe went to New York City desiring to write plays, but not finding much success. He then earned an M.A. degree in English from Harvard University, then took a job teaching at New York University. Wolfe turned to fiction since his early work as a playwright had failed to gain acceptance from theater producers. He was teaching at Washington Square College of New York University when he began work on the novel.

Spending part of his time teaching in New York, and part of his time in London and Paris, Wolfe turned out a long manuscript over several years. Historians note that Scribner's editors knew they had an outstanding novel on their hands, but did not know the work would become monumental. It give fame to a shaggy bear of a man destined to be damned and praised for his total recall of events of childhood which he compressed into readable prose, some say with the help of his famous literary editor Maxwell Perkins. Perkins' effort and influence are disputed by some literary critics, but remain part of the folklore surrounding publication of the book.

When the book came out, critics declared Wolfe one of the new stars in the literary firmament. The book also made quite a splash in Wolfe's hometown of Asheville when it laid bare the travails of two supposedly fictional families, the Gants and the Pentlands, in the small town of Altamont. The pride, pettiness, greed, narrowness, and innermost secrets of Wolfe's thinly veiled families and local community for the era 1905 through the 1920s were all put down in equal detail for the world to see.

Wolfe, youngest of eight children born to William Oliver and Julia Westall Wolfe—two of Asheville's better-known citizens from the period 1880 to 1922, sailed into trouble at home amid triumph in New York because Asheville residents saw the Gants as the Wolfes and the Pentlands as the Westalls, with the supporting cast of characters as themselves.

When the storm broke, Tom called his mother to explain the role of a writer. She understood or, at least, said she did. So did others with literary backgrounds, but the experience was a bitter lesson. According to lore, the local literary society ladies couldn't wait to talk with fellow member Mabel Wolfe Wheaton, Tom's sister, to obtain her response to the book. Her reaction was to write her own book which she said would tell the real story of the Wolfe family. Tom's mother followed with her version of the Wolfe family story.

Raleigh newspaper editor Jonathan Daniels, a classmate of Wolfe's at Chapel Hill and later ambassador to Mexico, did think Wolfe used his family harshly in the novel.

Mrs. J. M. Roberts, Wolfe's high school English teacher and mentor, was hurt by a reference to her husband as "stupid and inept." He was headmaster of the private North State School where Wolfe was a pupil after public elementary school. Wolfe wrote to her: "I can only assure you that my book is a work of fiction, and that no person, act, or event has been deliberately or consciously described." That didn't still the uproar.

Residents of Asheville read the book eagerly but refused to purchase copies. Borrowed copies were in great demand, instead. Asheville's residents were titillated and shocked by Tom's exposure of himself, his family, and fellow townsmen. It was *scandalous*, they said. Even his friends and supporters later admitted it was years before they could read "that book," as they called it, with some objectivity.

There is no question that Wolfe was quite an observer of the human comedy. And there is no question that he was an outstanding recorder of events as they affected him. The problem, said the critics, was that Wolfe gave equal importance to everything that came along in his stream of consciousness. Therein lies the controversy in literary circles over the work of Thomas Wolfe, author. He did have some misgivings about the work, according to biographers and his own writings, but he continued to deny the novel was autobiographical in a literal sense. He told his family and friends the novel was autobiographical in its treatment—more in line with drama. Over and over again he said fiction is not fact, but fiction is fact arranged and charged with purpose.

Notwithstanding Wolfe's disclaimers, the Asheville populace didn't know the difference and they were furious. Townspeople continued the drumbeat of damnation: How could Tom have done this to his family and Asheville? Indeed, how could he? Wolfe was the offspring of two prominent families, wealthy in relative terms for those days, as well as a member of the staid and conservative First Presbyterian Church. As a graduate of a private school, deemed brilliant by those who knew him, tutored by his favorite teacher and a freshman at the university at sixteen, Wolfe was a rising star in his beloved Asheville.

Young Thomas went to the university at Chapel Hill to be a dramatist. This was his education, his training, his world. He became a playwright turned novelist when his plays did not sell, and this nuance was lost on the home folks. But it explains the style and substance of his work. His people missed the point, and the prophet was without honor in his hometown.

Even now, people who remember the Wolfes, and who were far enough on the sidelines not to have been mentioned in the book, say

Tom would have been physically attacked if he had ridden the train back into town right after publication. In Western North Carolina's mountains even today, the public does not take kindly to literary license in the name of drama. Libraries, schools, theater, and the arts still tread lightly lest controversy again be visited upon Asheville.

The *Look Homeward, Angel* controversy lasted into the mid-1960s before Tom's brother, Fred, would stand in the auditorium of Pack Memorial Library in downtown Asheville and declare, "Tom, you can come home again. You are home." It was an emotional moment in literary history as Fred Wolfe, the model of one of the characters in the novel, signaled the forgiveness and pride he and his family felt toward their brother, however posthumously. Fred, the last surviving sibling in the family, served as their spokesman.

The families and fellow townspeople about whom Wolfe wrote are all gone now. My Old Kentucky Home, as the Wolfe boarding house on Spruce Street was named, is now the Wolfe Memorial, open to visitors. Across the street from the rooming and boarding house is one of Asheville's high-rise hotels. The site of W. O. Wolfe's marble shop on Pack Square, the place where the angel stood for so long in front of "Gant's" shop, as Thomas's father, W. O. Wolfe was known in the play, is now a beloved historical element of Asheville's ongoing rehabilitation and beautification of Pack Square. It has been preserved intact, and years ago became part of a downtown bank building, which is now across from the Akzona-Biltmore Building.

The angel is in Oakdale Cemetery in Hendersonville, some twenty miles south of Asheville, while a replica stands in front of Pack Place, the old library, now an arts and entertainment complex. W. O. Wolfe sold the angel to a family named Johnson, and it graces their family burial plot. The city of Hendersonville built an iron fence around the statue to prevent vandalism and theft after a Wolfe fan tried to carry the heavy statue away in the night and it fell over, breaking fingers on one of the angel's hands. Asheville tried to obtain the angel for display, but the Johnson family survivors and city turned down the request. A historical marker reminds motorists on US 64 West that the famous Wolfe angel is a few yards away, within viewing distance of drivers. Hendersonville's Chamber of Commerce used photographs of the angel on the cover of its tourist booklet for years, and each year hundreds of visitors journey to see the angel. Henderson County high school English classes once honored Thomas Wolfe on his birthday by regularly gathering at the angel for a ceremony.

For many years, the Flat Rock Playhouse south of Hendersonville, now the State Theater, had an annual production of the stage play, *Look Homeward, Angel*, to the delight of summer audiences. Before he passed away, Fred Wolfe came to Flat Rock to see the play and to officially dedicate Thomas Wolfe Drive on the theater grounds. Both the Asheville Community Theater and the University of North Carolina at Asheville have mounted productions of the play that have been well received.

Thomas Wolfe lies in the family plot in the rolling hills of Riverside Cemetery in Asheville, overlooking the French Broad River. Mrs. J. M. Roberts, Wolfe's mentor-teacher, and the one person in his life who he claimed had brought beauty and order out of that hell of chaos, greed, and cheap values that characterized Asheville in his era, is gone too. The wellspring of his genius, Asheville, is now a metropolitan area with all of the social, economic, and physical problems associated with modern society. It is crossed by freeways, loops, cuts through ridges, and a mishmash of new architecture. To some, the hell of chaos, greed, and cheap values remain. But October, Wolfe's favorite month in his native land, is still the most beautiful time of the year as the entire countryside turns golden. Wolfe loved how sunlight burns the thick green hillsides into brilliant hues of blazing fall colors. He loved the warmth of days turned drowsy, and the haze of autumn. Of course, he wrote about it in his novel, *Of Time and the River*.

Wolfe's beloved month of October still arrives the way he knew it as thousands upon thousands of tourists crowd hotels, motels, and highways to see the leaves change color in the Blue Ridge and Great Smokies. The Plott hounds of the mountains still bay in the moonlight as they track their prey in the crisp autumn air. October gives way to the gray of winter, when occasionally a dusting of snow turns Wolfe's golden world of Altamont into a white fairyland; the people flock to town to see this winter wonderland, too. Springs and summers bring more people to Wolfe's home. And the river, the French Broad, still flows in its rugged course over rocks and boulders northward into eternity.

Tom Wolfe did come home again. He's home in Asheville, his beloved Altamont. And he is forgiven.

First Automobile Trips Over the Smokies Were Major Adventures

A fellow named Jack Huff of Knoxville, Tennessee, is credited with making the first automobile drive over the Smokies. He and three companions followed a new road, now US 441, up the Tennessee side to Newfound Gap and then down the other side into North Carolina, following a logging railroad built to transport timber from the Newfound Gap area to a sawmill at Smokemont. Huff's success at coming down the North Carolina side over boulders and logs in 1930 prompted a young Bryson City pharmacist named Kelly "Doc" Bennett to take up the challenge of driving up the North Carolina side to Newfound Gap and down the new road to Gatlinburg.

It was a challenge Doc Bennett couldn't resist. Owner of Bryson City's leading drugstore and a mountain man, Bennett also presided over the town's informal morning coffee club where townsmen discussed politics and the news of the day, and took part in a little "funnin'" at the expense of club members who told of their gaffs hunting bear, fishing, or hiking in the mountains. When the subject got around to Huff's feat, Bennett couldn't resist saying that if Huff and three companions could drive down through the wilderness, he could drive up and over in one day with just one companion—fellow townsman Ray Smith—riding shotgun instead of three other men.

Mark it down, the North Carolina side of the Smokies from Newfound Gap to Cherokee was real wilderness. Eagles and other birds of prey soared over the ridges and deep coves, while on the ground there were concentrated areas of growth, called laurel and rhododendron hells, so thick hunters could walk on top of the canopy of boughs. If caught in one of these hells, a walker could become completely lost and stuck, so dark and tangled they were within. Even the logging railroad only went so far. It was wild land. But then, mountain-man Bennett, friend of Horace Kephart, wasn't exactly an amateur in the ridges and coves of the Smokies. He'd hunted, fished, and lived his life in the rugged land of the Cherokee. He also was a leading citizen of Bryson City where he became a legend for his civic work, years in the North Carolina General Assembly, and service as mayor.

Bennett also was a leader in North Carolina for the Good Roads movement. From 1917, the year of his initial term in the General Assembly, until his death in 1974, Doc Bennett was known as the "Apostle of the Smokies." He was the most influential and civic-minded citizen Swain County has ever had. A sign in Bryson City proclaimed: "Ask Bennett, He Knows." More often than not, he did.

His idea for the trip from North Carolina to Tennessee via Newfound Gap was not the first time Doc Bennett had scored a first in travel. His first encounter for Good Roads came in 1905 when he led a visitor to the Smokies, John Ford, on a trip that is now called "The Last Buggy Ridge Across the Smokies."

Ford paid Bennett a dollar a day for an incredible journey from Bryson City to Robbinsville to Rymers Ferry on the Little Tennessee through a gap in the Smokies, down into Tennessee to the Hardin Place, and on into Maryville. There they put the team and buggy in a livery stable and traveled by train to Knoxville for a visit. Returning to Maryville, they went up the right prong of the Little Pigeon River to Pigeon Forge. Reaching Gatlinburg, they followed the old Col. Will Thomas Road leading to Whittier by way of Indian Gap on the state line high in the Smokies and on down through Smokemont and Cherokee. That trip took one month and three days on the trail. Bennett took the $1 a day he made from escorting Ford, added some from his savings, and purchased his first drugstore in Bryson City. "You might say I got started by conducting the first tourist on the first tour of the Great Smokies," he said later.

The automobile trip would prove to be as challenging as the buggy trip. Without fanfare Doc Bennett and Ray Smith left Bryson City and drove the eighteen miles to the end of the dirt road at Smokemont in his Chevrolet roadster. In a little over an hour, the easy part was over.

John Parris, a native son of the Smokies who had an outstanding career as a war correspondent during world War II and later became associate editor of the *Asheville Citizen-Times*, wrote that when Bennett reached Smokemont and announced to the Champion Paper loggers he was going to drive to Newfound Gap, they merely laughed. One logger, Parris reported, told Bennett that he'd never make across the three forks of the 'Lufty (Oconaluftee River), and that ain't much more than a quarter of a mile away."

"Is that so?" Bennett laughed. "Why, I'll be in Gatlinburg before supper time." He wasn't, but the tale of Bennett's trip is now part of the lore and legend of the Smokies. With the loggers agape, Bennett—confident to the point of cockiness—waved and the pair roared off into the wilderness.

With one tank of gasoline and no blankets or food, Bennett and Smith found trouble soon after they started up the right prong of the Oconaluftee. The idea was to drive up the riverbed, cross to solid ground on the other side, and follow the railroad to the top. This is how it was done with horse and wagon in earlier times. Alas, Bennett and Smith were driving a Chevy roadster, not a horse and wagon.

At the fork the logger talked about, they struck a shelving rock and bounced astride a boulder in the river. The car was hung up. It took the two men more than an hour of pushing and shoving in the icy water before they freed the roadster. On the other side was the logging railroad; they intended to drive as far as it went to the gap. There was only one problem: To reach the railroad from the river they would have to climb a high bank. Bennett came prepared for the task. He brought a pick and shovel plus block and tackle. They literally built a road up the bank, hooked the car to the block and tackle, and hauled the car up the path to the railroad bed by hand. That took more precious time.

All logging railroads built by the timber companies of that era, Champion Paper no exception, were narrow gauge or less than 56½ inches from rail to rail. This meant the wheels of the car had to be outside the two rails, which was rough on the cross ties. Champion had not used this section in some time, and the ties were in bad shape. Not only were ties skewed in some places, many were missing. Whenever the gaps between ties were too great, the car's wheels would go down, and the springs of the car would rest on the rails, leaving the wheels to spin. Bennett and Smith would then get out, jack up the car, push it forward until it gained traction on the next tie, and then move anywhere from three to twenty feet before they had to repeat the process.

They approached a trestle on the abandoned railway only to find some of the cross ties missing, leaving gaps to the ground below. They found some spare ties along the roadbed, so they dragged them to the trestle and repaired the gaps before proceeding safely across.

Now they were making time, bouncing along the ties in a bone-rattling ride up the flanks of the gap. That is, until they came to a place where the rail bed had sunk into a morass. Bennett later told his friends, the car kept burying its front in the mud, and he and Smith kept throwing rocks in the car's path and using the block and tackle attached to a tree to pull the car out of the mud. "It looked like we were stuck for good," Bennett is quoted by Parris in one of his columns. "But Smith put the car in gear, full throttle, then jumped out and helped me pull on the rope that was fixed to a tree. We pulled her out."

Another mile up the railroad and they encountered an old logging camp. They breezed through the camp's open clearing and on the other side regained the railroad. Again it was more rocks between the ties, more block and tackle, more tugging on the rope tied to a tree to go another half mile. The trip was becoming a construction project and endurance test of man and machine against the idea of following an abandoned narrow gauge railroad through the last wilderness in eastern America to make good on a brag at a drugstore soda fountain.

It was around 5:30 in the afternoon when they reached another logging camp. They had barely traveled four miles from where they started at Smokemont. Today travelers on the same road, now US 441—the main road from Cherokee to Newfound Gap to Gatlinburg, cover the four miles in six to seven minutes if traffic is light. The Chevy roadster rolled into a clearing where Clive Beck and a crew from Champion Paper were building a camp for the firm's timber cruisers as they started a new lead next to Deep Creek near Indian Gap.

The hour was late and Bennett and Smith knew it, but they pressed on only to encounter another roadblock just three hundred yards from the camp. It seems earlier loggers had tossed hemlock branches into a small stream to aid in crossing, and silt had built up. The car again sank up to the hub caps. It was a weary repeat of previous events on the rocky road to the top, only worse. Once again they piled rocks under all the wheels, tied the block and tackle to a big stump, and prepared to haul. Smith then tried to start the car with Bennett hauling on the rope at the stump. The car didn't want to start. Smith finally got the car started, moved forward, jerked the rope, and Bennett found himself tumbling head over heels into the muck. They had spent three hours at that spot and traveled six feet toward their destination. It was getting dark and beginning to snow. They plowed forward another few hundred yards before they left the track to climb a bank. To climb the bank, they had to gather more cross ties and build another stairway for the car. It took fifteen ties, Bennett later told friends, to build that stairway. Alas, the car bogged down on the stairway. They were stuck again on the cusp of nightfall and nowhere near the new road to Gatlinburg at Newfound Gap. The prize was so close yet so far.

It was decision time. Cold, hungry, and worn out, the two men decided not to freeze to death, so they walked back down the roadbed the three hundred yards to Clive Beck's new camp and spent the night out of the snow and cold. As they backtracked to the camp, it began to snow harder. They had made the right decision.

The next morning they were up at 7:30 and on their way to the car. With the help of the loggers from the camp, they heaved the roadster out of the muck, up the incline, and onto the roadbed. It was four miles to Newfound Gap. This next phase of the trip went smoothly. No more obstacles as the roadbed was good. They reached their goal, the Gap, then Bennett fairly flew down the new road from Newfound Gap and was in Sevierville an hour later.

He had made good on his boast—he made the first trip across the Smokies from the North Carolina side in an automobile. He and Ray Smith went uphill the hard way, under their own steam, rather than using gravity's help to more or less roll downhill as had Jack Huff and his companions. Bennett came back a hero to the folks in Bryson City in 1930. Of course, he was behind his own schedule on this one. In that bragging session with his friends over coffee at the local drugstore, he had set himself a timetable by saying he'd make it over the mountain by noon. The trip actually took about twenty-four hours. Town folks didn't care. Doc did what he said he was going to do.

Auto travel came late to the Smokies when you considering the rest of the country was well on its way to being crisscrossed with paved roads in February 1930, when Bennett and Smith made their epic trip. Today thousands of automobiles travel US 441 each day with nary a thought that once upon a time it was a rickety railroad track through the wilderness that Horace Kephart called the "back of beyond."

Kelly "Doc" Bennett had made his point—North Carolina needed more good roads one third into the twentieth century. He lived to see a paved road to Newfound Gap and the dedication of the Great Smokies as a national treasure and park, another goal of the civic leader and pharmacist from Bryson City. Old Doc also knew how to make good on a soda fountain brag.

Church by the Wildwood

There's a church in the valley by the wildwood, no lovelier spot in the dale . . ."

Dr. William Pitts wrote those words in his famous old hymn, "The Church by the Wildwood," many years ago. It is doubtful he had the wildwood of Davidson River valley in mind, but there is a church in Western North Carolina that evokes the memory of Dr. Pitts' hymn. It is English Chapel. Most people who travel US 276 from the village of Pisgah Forest to Sliding Rock, the Cradle of Forestry, Wagon Road Gap, and the Blue Ridge Parkway are unaware of the only organized church within the boundary of a national forest in the United States.

The story of English Chapel goes back to before the Civil War; it goes back to before George Vanderbilt's purchase of the farms, hamlets, and lands that now make up Pisgah National Forest; it goes back to the days of circuit-riding Methodist ministers who came to the Blue Ridge mountains after the Rev. Samuel Asbury to carry on the work of Methodism's founder, John Wesley.

Located about a mile and a half inside Pisgah National Forest from the intersection of NC 280 and US 64 where US 276 begins its twisting, winding way from the village of Pisgah Forest to the Blue Ridge Parkway, the church is hidden from view in a glade across the Davidson River. It is reached by a bridge on the west side of the road less than one hundred yards from the Pisgah Forest Ranger Station. The chapel may also be reached from the Davidson River Campground operated by the Cradle of Forestry in America Interpretative Association, Inc.

Back in the 1860s, when English Chapel was founded as a Methodist church by the Rev. F. F. English, a circuit-riding Methodist minister in the western counties of the state well before the Civil War, there were a number of small farms and settlements in what is now the national forest. These farms and settlements grew up along the river and the Cherokee trading path which led from the border of Virginia along the Blue Ridge to Estatoe (now under the waters of Lake Jocassee) in South Carolina, one of the Cherokee's regional capitals.

When Reverend English settled in the Davidson River section with his wife, who came from the French Broad River Valley, he obtained land for the price of $5 from his father-in-law, Strawbridge Young, one of the area's early settlers, in order to build the chapel. The original building was wooden, built from lumber the Reverend English sawed at his mill at Avery's Creek. The chapel was used one Sunday a month by the Methodists, the Sunday that the circuit rider was there, and other Sundays by other Christian denominations. If at any time the chapel falls into disuse, it reverts to the English family, according to the deed.

When George Vanderbilt made settlers in the valley and Pink Beds an offer for their land that they could not refuse, the chapel remained an enclave within the estate for worshipers who came from as far away as Brevard, Pisgah Forest, and other hamlets along the Davidson River.

In the 1940s, the wooden 1860s chapel needed repair, so church members gathered river rock from the nearby Davidson and along with stones brought to the site by visitors from other states, built the present rock chapel. The chapel still has Davidson River and Pisgah Forest families as members. Each Sunday during the summer, visitors staying at the Davidson River Campground attend services too. The minister who serves as pastor for English Chapel members is a modern equivalent of the circuit-riding Methodist ministers of bygone days. He serves another small church west of nearby Brevard. At the end of the 9:30 service at English Chapel, he goes to a 10:30 service at the other church.

To those who visit on Sundays, the hymn's verses about the church in the wildwood provide memories of the pioneers of an earlier era who settled the wilderness lands of the Cherokee, and who never forgot divine guidance. In the quiet of a Sunday morning with the rushing water outside, the beauty of the glade and the hills nearby, each worshiper, "outlanders" included, may claim to "wing my way to the mansions of light" in sacred worship.

The church by the wildwood really exists, even today.

NOTE: The chapel is about twenty miles on US 64 West from Hendersonville, twenty-four miles from Asheville, fourteen miles from the Asheville Regional Airport via NC 280, and three miles from Brevard.

I'm My Own Grandfather and She's Her Own Grandmother

Once upon a time there was a country music hit called, "I'm My Own Grandpa." The song created quite a stir in the 1950s. To the world outside of the mountains and country music, being one's own grandfather was considered impossible. A mountain lawyer and judge from Waynesville nigh unto the Smokies disputed the naysayers by citing a case he had in Macon County where one of the principals was not only his own grandfather but a widow in the same case was also her own grandmother.

Judge Felix Alley delighted in telling this story when he rode the circuit of courts in Western North Carolina as a lawyer and later as one of the most distinguished jurists in the mountains. He included the story in a book called, *Random Thoughts and the Musings of a Mountaineer*, now out of print, and most likely found in the rare book sections of libraries.

Relationships in the mountains are often complex because isolation caused women and men to marry within their immediate neighborhoods, villages, ridges, coves, and hamlets. They often

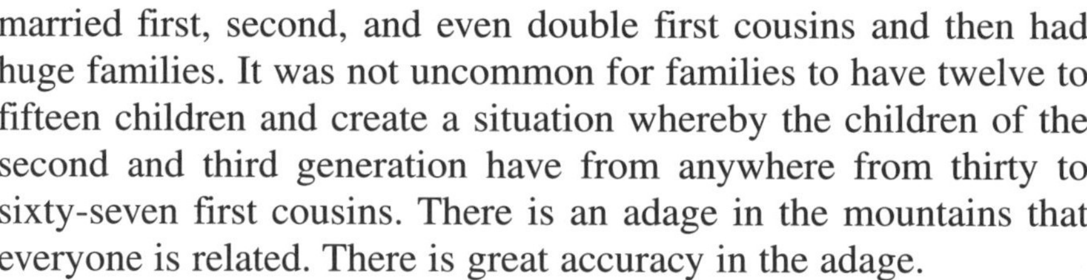

married first, second, and even double first cousins and then had huge families. It was not uncommon for families to have twelve to fifteen children and create a situation whereby the children of the second and third generation have from anywhere from thirty to sixty-seven first cousins. There is an adage in the mountains that everyone is related. There is great accuracy in the adage.

It happened, Judge Alley said, when a widower married the daughter of a widow who then married the son of the widower, and both had children. Lawyer Alley was called upon to unravel the relationships for some now-obscure legal reason. However, he loved to regale young lawyers on the saddlebag court circuit with the story to illustrate his legal mind. As a judge he noted and advocated the strong opinion that common sense and logic must often prevail over the technicality or letter of the law, at least in his courtroom.

In the culture of the mountains stories are told among families or different groups to make a point or send a message indirectly, so there won't be confrontation between the parties involved. Those in the law profession are no exception to this tradition. As judges and lawyers traveled together on the circuits, they found the need to entertain each other at night in the taverns where they lodged. Members like Judge Alley, whose long experience and preeminence made his words almost as respected as the law itself, told and retold certain stories to educate the younger men as to the proper and accepted way to go about doing things, as well as to establish and maintain his authority. The young lawyers—and old hands, too—got the point about what was expected of them in their dealings before ever actually entering the mountain courtrooms to do business before Judge Alley. More often than not, the stories were told while lawyers and judges sat around a table at a hotel or boarding house the evening before court convened.

Here is the fascinating story of tangled family relations the judge repeated over and over until it became part of the folklore of the mountains:

> Some years ago Joe Calloway, with his wife and a grown-up son, named Bill, lived near Highlands in Macon County. In the same community there lived a man by the name of Reuben Smith, who had a wife and a grown-up daughter whose name was Sallie.
>
> Eventually Mrs. Calloway died and left surviving her

old man, Joe, her husband, and their son, Bill. About the same time old man Smith died, leaving surviving him his widow and their daughter, Sallie.

A little later on, old man Joe Calloway married Sallie, the daughter of the widow, and shortly thereafter Bill, old man Calloway's son, married the widow Smith.

As the result of these marriages Bill became the father-in-law of his own father, because his father had married the daughter of Bill's wife; but Bill also became the step-father of his own father, because his father had married Bill's step-daughter. By the same token, Sallie became the mother-in-law of her own mother because her mother had married Sallie's step-son.

Now, old man Calloway was Bill's father; but he was also Bill's step-son and his son-in-law at the same time because he had married the daughter of Bill's wife. And Bill's wife, the former widow Smith, was Sallie's mother; but she was also the step-daughter and the daughter-in-law of her daughter Sallie because she had married the son of Sallie's husband.

Sometime after these marriages a daughter was born to the old man Calloway and Sallie, and they named her Mary. At about the same time a son was born to Bill Calloway and his wife, the former widow Smith, and they gave him the name of Sam. Now Mary and Bill were sister and brother because they were children of the same father; but Mary being the sister of Bill, was also the aunt of Bill's son Sam. Sam and Sallie were brother and sister also because they were the children of the same mother; but Sam, although he was Sallie's brother, was likewise the uncle of Sallie's daughter Mary. Bill, however, being both the father-in-law and step-father of Sallie, became the grand-father of Sallie's daughter Mary because Bill was the husband of Mary's grand-mother, the former widow Smith; while Sallie, as the mother-in-law and step-mother of Bill, became the grand-mother of Bill's son Sam, because Sallie was the wife of Sam's grand-father, old man Calloway. So Bill was Mary's brother and her grand-father at one and the same time, and Sallie was Sam's sister and his grand-mother at the same time.

Now Bill's son was Bill's father's brother-in-law because he was the brother of old man Joe Calloway's wife; but he was also Bill's uncle because he was the brother of Bill's step-mother; and Mary was also Bill's step-sister because she was the daughter of Bill's step-mother;

> but Mary was likewise Bill's grand-child because she was the grand-child of Bill's wife. So Bill's wife became Bill's grand-mother, because Bill was his wife's husband and her grand-child at one and the same time, as the husband of one's grand-mother is necessarily his grand-father, Bill became his own grand-father.
>
> By virtue of the same relationship Sallie's daughter Mary was Sallie's mother's sister-in-law because she was the sister of the widow Smith's husband; but she was also Sallie's aunt because she was the sister of Sallie's step-father; but Sam was also Sallie's step-brother because he was the son of Sallie's step-father. But he was likewise Sallie's grand-child because he was the grand-child of Sallie's husband. So Sallie's husband became her grand-father because Sallie was her husband's wife and his grand-child at one and the same time, and as the wife of one's grand-father is necessarily her grand-mother, Sallie became her own grand-mother.

Of course, in the glow of the fireplace, country cooking, and "medicine," listeners became lost early in the story but enjoyed it, which, of course, led to other tales. A song and story about "My Own Grandpa (or Grandma)" is not as farfetched as visitors to the mountains might think. How Judge Alley loved to tell this story! It now is part of mountain folklore as well as being true.

The Little People or "Spirits"

Thousands of people each year visit Hickory Nut Gorge and Chimney Rock, fifteen miles south of Asheville on NC 74, and twelve miles east of Hendersonville on US 64. Few of them, though, have ever heard about the little people or "spirits" who are said to inhabit the great heights above the gorge and rock.

In yesteryear, the tale of the little people was a ritual on cold winter nights in the coves of the Blue Ridge when the wind howled outside log cabins. Inside father or grandfather sat before a crackling hickory, oak, or chestnut log fire, and told stories calculated to hold the attention of the young-uns. This tale of the spirits comes to us from a number of sources, including newspaper articles dated as far back as 1808, stories written in 1811, and early Cherokee tales. The earliest remembrance is in the oral history of the Cherokee long before settlers moved into the southern highlands.

The legend of Chimney Rock has attracted storytellers and people interested in folktales ever since the Cherokee version was translated. Various versions have cropped up since, but the essential story remains the same, a story that has believers.

The Cherokee tale goes back to early days in Cherokee history when the *Tomahaitan*, or Cherokee, heard about the wonders of tobacco from a wandering stranger from the eastern part of the great land. Naming it *tsolugeh*, or tobacco weed, the Cherokee wanted some for their great ceremonial stone pipes. How to obtain the weed consumed many hours of discussion in the long houses of the Cherokee until a young warrior volunteered to travel to the big water (the Atlantic Ocean) near where tobacco was grown. He told the Cherokee leaders he would return with *tsolugeh* for the ceremonial pipes.

He left on the trip, never to return. His route was supposed to be through the present Hickory Nut Gorge. When the warrior did not return within the allotted time, a Cherokee mystic volunteered to make what apparently was a hazardous trip. Cunning, the mystic decided, would be more valuable than strength on the trip, so he turned himself into a mole to go through the Gorge. In so doing, he managed to evade the spirits who reportedly inhabited the Gorge. The mystic didn't bring back much tobacco as a mole, but on a later trip as a hummingbird he did manage to bring back enough of the fragrant weed for the pipes. The Cherokee elders were pleased. Once more the mystic undertook the trip, this time as a whirlwind. The whirlwind roared through the Gorge, removing all of the growth on the side of the cliffs, overturning huge boulders, and remaking the terrain of the Gorge. The mystic also drove out the spirits, and ever after the Cherokee used Hickory Nut Gorge to travel to the Outer Banks to obtain tobacco, which eventually was grown in abundance in the mountains. The mystic also found the body of the young warrior in a pool in the Gorge and returned him to life in the land of his forefathers.

It wasn't until much, much later that the Rev. George Newton, a Presbyterian teacher who later organized the Newton Academy on Biltmore Avenue in Asheville, told about an 1806 story in the *Raleigh Gazette and Register* which describes an actual sighting of the little people or spirits by one Patsy Reeves and her children, all of whom lived about three-fourths of a mile below Chimney Rock in the early 1800s.

The Reeves children saw apparitions of human beings around Chimney Rock and reported the sighting to their mother. Mrs. Reeves, a widow, didn't believe them, but when she went to the place where the children could see the spirits, she told friends there were thousands of people in white robes gathering in the air near the rock. She became afraid and called for help. On her second cry for help, one Robert Siercy came, and he, too, saw the assembled spirits on the mountain. He was quite shaken by the experience, according to reports of the day. The spirits swirling about looked like men, women, and children in robes, he later said. Nothing Mr. Siercy ever saw before or again was quite like the spirits he observed that day at Chimney Rock from the cotton patch near the Reeves cabin.

In 1848, the Cherokee legend was again mentioned, in one of its numerous retellings. When the Reverend Newton explained it, he did so by telling his listeners that the spirits were an optical illusion so common in the mountains. People's belief in "haints" or spirits might make them more apt to see such things. Also, distance and light contribute to these very real manifestations. It is now known that the mountains contain some very mysterious natural elements, like strange gases that rise from the earth, which are known to possibly cause such phenomena. Reverend Newton explained it quite well for his audiences. But still, the spirits, or little people, as some called them, continued as legend because those who inhabited the coves and hollows often beheld other events bordering on the unexplainable.

"Haints" or haunts are part of the woof and weave in the fabric of mountain culture. In the dark forests, isolated balds, great heights, coves, ridges, hollows, and roaring rivers, one can almost feel the spirits—or so both Cherokees and settlers agreed. It was ever so, yesterday and even today. Hidden back in the plateau above Chimney Rock is a real lost colony; the Cherokee did go through the Gorge to the land below the escarpment for tobacco; the paths did lead to the Big Water; Rumbling Bald across the valley from Chimney Rock really does rumble; the pools on the side of the mountain above Lake Lure do seem bottomless; and far away to the north at Brown Mountain there are still unexplainable lights.

To the Scots-Irish and German settlers who entered the hills from Ireland, Scotland, and Germany to live after the Cherokee Removal, the spirits and little people, were very real in their lives. In the blue haze of summer around Chimney Rock, there are still those who swear they've seen those mysterious apparitions of the past. Someday, they say, others will see them too.

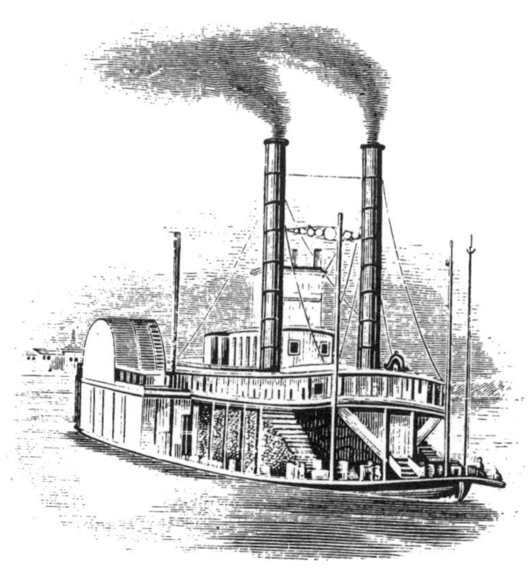

The Mountain Lily

Every time Congress passes its annual Rivers and Harbors Bill, folks in the Blue Ridge Mountains of Western North Carolina harken back to the day when they boasted of "the highest steamship line in the world." Flagship of the line was *The Mountain Lily*, a ninety-foot-long, two-deck, side-wheeler equipped with two twelve-horsepower steam engines and accommodations for one hundred passengers as well as space for U.S. Mail and freight.

She was quite a river boat.

The French Broad Steam Boat Company was a grandiose scheme to make money that was linked with the annual "Pork Barrel" bill offered in Congress. Which came first, the pork-barrel idea, development of the French Broad River west of Asheville, or the steamship promotion, isn't known for sure; but promoters left few stones unturned in their attempt to create the golden days of river boating twenty-two hundred feet above sea level.

It began in 1876, when Robert B. Vance, United States representative from the mountain district of Western North Carolina, managed to put a bill through Congress appropriating $25,000 to clear the channel and deepen the French Broad River from the mouth of the Oklawaha as far as Brevard. Those who favored the bill claimed it would make the French Broad River navigable all the way from Asheville to Brevard, a distance of forty miles. The old Cherokee name Oklawaha was written into the bill because its sponsors felt the name Mud Creek undignified.

There were protests to the idea, even in the mountains. Vance's younger brother, Zeb Vance, Civil War governor of North Carolina and then a United States senator, violently opposed the bill. Other opposition was by Sen. Allen Thurman of Ohio, who was so vehement in his opposition that he declared during debate, "Why, gentlemen, even a catfish couldn't navigate the French Broad River from the mouth of Mud Creek to Brevard."

Despite the acid comment by Senator Thurman and opposition by Senator Vance, the bill introduced by Rep. Robert Vance of Asheville for his relative and Confederate Army comrade, Col. Sidney Vance Pickens, passed both House and Senate. The enterprising Colonel Pickens, a prominent lawyer and leading citizen of Hendersonville who served with "Fighting Joe" Wheeler's Cavalry during the Civil War, operated the first street railway in his mountain town. It was a small car drawn by mules. Colonel Pickens dreamed of a transportation empire, and while two mules and a small car were a humble beginning, a steamboat line would open all sorts of possibilities for surface and water transportation.

The $25,000 appropriated became the first federal project for improvement of the French Broad River. The project was also unusual because, the government reported, it was the only development on the whole Tennessee River system "that was not carried on with the expectation of contributing to navigation on the main stream as well as on the tributary."

Work scheduled on the French Broad River by the U.S. Army Engineers was some ninety miles above the head of navigation at Leadvale, Tennessee. To have connected Asheville with Leadvale was out of the question—the river falls an average of 13.4 feet per mile between the two towns. Few people gave this much thought, and the army engineers moved their wagon train into the valley in 1875 to begin work on the French Broad River. Their work continued until 1880.

The channel of the river was dredged and cleared of debris. Some of the debris were stumps and trunks of trees lodged in the river for centuries gone by. Where underlying rock formed shoals, it was blasted out. Even these efforts failed to deepen the river in places, so the army engineers narrowed the river by building jetties along the banks to make it deeper. The project was like any public works in that before it was completed the cost was more than double the original appropriation.

With the completion of the channel deepening in 1880, the next logical step for Colonel Pickens was to propose a steamship line. He was joined by two other men who showed more vision than navigation experience: Jonathan Williams, two-time mayor of Hendersonville and politician; and Albert Cannon, known to everyone in the mountain country as "Squire Cannon," a leading farmer and promoter of agriculture and the Commissioner of Agriculture for North Carolina for a number of years. Squire Cannon's farm was at Horse Shoe, a place that played an important role in the steamboat days.

The three men went about their task with dispatch. In the records of Corporations of Henderson County, Book 1, page 3, there is the following:

> We, Jonathan Williams, Albert Cannon and Sidney V. Pickens, do hereby form a private corporation under and in conformity with the provisions of an Act of the General Assembly of North Carolina. Organized for the purpose of building and running a steamboat on the French Broad River from some point near Brevard to any point said Corporation may think practical on said river of any of its tributaries not lower than Asheville. The purpose of the Corporation is to carry freight and passengers and, if necessary, the United States Mail.

The charter of the French Broad Steam Boat Company noted "capital stock of this corporation is $4,000 with the right to increase it to the limit of the law." The stock was divided into 160 shares with par value per share of $25. Jonathan Williams subscribed to 4 shares, Albert Cannon to 2 shares, and Colonel Pickens to 4 shares.

All of this took place September 25, 1880. What kind of winter the three gentlemen from Henderson County had isn't noted, but it wasn't until May 6, 1881, that county records show some activity by the three men whose total investment was $250. On this date they purchased three-quarters of an acre of land from Richard Ledbetter, "a certain parcel of land lying or being on the East bank of the French Broad River," to serve as the landing dock for passengers and freight, and as a ticket office.

Spring in the mountains is a wonderful time and the year 1881 was no exception. The idea of an all-day outing, picnic, and barbecue sponsored by the French Broad Steam Boat Company made it even better.

All over Henderson, Transylvania, Buncombe, Polk, and adjoining counties, men in wagons and buggies traveled in a grand public-relations effort. They tacked up signs and posters on every crossroad sign, tree, post, and outbuilding. Boys and men on horseback with saddlebags stuffed with handbills rode country roads handing out notices at every farmhouse, while small boys in the towns and villages left handbills on every doorstep or front porch.

The brightly colored posters extolled the public:

Come One, Come All!

All Day Picnic and Barbecue at Horse Shoe, Henderson County!
Everybody Invited, Men, Women and Children!

As the people stopped to read the advertisements, they became interested. There would be plenty to eat and drink including, for those who liked it, "hard stuff." One of the lures was band music and speech making. The advance men for Colonel Pickens and friends did their job well.

By wagon, buggy, horseback, ox cart, and rowboat, the people swarmed into the village of Horse Shoe for the picnic sponsored by the French Broad Steam Boat Company. Never in the history of Henderson County had such a crowd gathered. A brass band played all day. When everybody had their fill of eating and drinking, the orators took over.

Speech making was an art in the mountains in those days, and the silver-tongued orators extolling the merits of the French Broad Steam Boat Company were at their best. They told about the company that had been organized; they told about the wonderful steamboat that was going to be built. It would run up and down the French Broad River from Asheville to Brevard, they said. Other boats would be built as soon as possible. Prosperity such as had never been dreamed would come to the fertile French Broad River Valley!

Brevard and Hendersonville would grow into large cities. Horse Shoe would become a thriving center of commerce as industry built on the banks of the French Broad River. The steamboat would provide cheap transportation for both passengers and goods. The cheap freight rates by water would open up new markets for manufactured goods as well as produce grown on the farms of the valley.

A new day was dawning! All the people had to do was sign for stock at only $25 a share. Everybody became so worked up by the glowing picture of prosperity just around the river bend that all of the shares in the company were subscribed that day, and the public clamored for more.

Colonel Pickens, Albert Cannon, and Jonathan Williams were men of action. Soon after the picnic they ordered construction started on a steamboat. Records are a bit hazy as to who was in charge, a Captain Arverill from Norfolk, Virginia, or a Mr. Wheat from Charleston, South Carolina, but work was begun on *The Mountain Lily* near the site of the French Broad Steam Boat Company ticket office at Horse Shoe.

As the boat took shape on the bank of the French Broad, it soon became apparent the builders knew what they were doing. It looked exactly like steamboats plying the waters of the Ohio and Mississippi. The boat was ninety feet long, with two decks and staterooms enough to accommodate one hundred passengers, and with space enough below decks to carry freight and mail.

Work continued through the spring and into August before *The Mountain Lily* was ready for launching. Invitations went to the elite of mountain society and they responded.

The men wore their Sunday suits. Some even wore swallow-tailed coats and tall beaver hats. The ladies were arrayed in their colorful party dresses, ribbons, bows, and ostrich-plume hats. The mountain people were in their plain garb, print dresses, and sun bonnets.

Below yards of bunting at riverside was *The Mountain Lily*, her two paddle wheels gleaming in the sun. Her two engines, each generating twelve horsepower of steam, had been installed. The boat's white paint was the whitest ever seen in the mountains. Her trim was as green as the fields next to the river.

The band played, speeches were made, and then Colonel Pickens announced the grand event—launching of *The Mountain Lily*. Workmen grabbed sledges and began the rally to knock the chocks from under the hull. As the finished boat started to slide into the river down the ways, the greased ramps upon which it was built, a pretty mountain girl smashed a bottle of champagne against the hull. "I christen thee *Mountain Lily*," she shouted. A cheer went up from the crowd as the boat splashed into the river water, August 2, 1881.

The boat's whistle echoed and reechoed up the coves and hollows of the nearby Blue Ridge. Crew members put out the gangplank, and the spectators came aboard for the maiden voyage: a short cruise down the river and back. Smoke poured from her stack, and the band played as she chugged downstream. It was a wonderful beginning that had the whole countryside talking.

Once the crowds left and the band stopped playing, *The Mountain Lily* was ready to begin earning a return on investment. That is when the troubles began. The French Broad River, despite the work of the army engineers, proved to be too shallow in some places and too narrow in others.

Accounts of *The Mountain Lily's* trips differ. Some folks say she did steam to Brevard several times, others say the boat only went upstream a few miles. For several years she was used mainly for excursions, parties, and moonlight dances.

On one of these daylight excursions, the story goes, *The Mountain Lily* hit a snag near King's Bridge and sank. She was on the bottom with part of her hull and all of her superstructure above water. It was decided not to raise and repair her because the river had reverted to its old ways of narrows, shoals, and snags. For a number of years the *Lily* sat in the water, prey to the ravages of time and little boys who loved to scamper along her tilted decks.

The boat, dream of three enterprising men, was finally dismantled. Salvage lumber from the *Lily* was used to build Riverside Baptist Church at Horse Shoe. Later when it was moved to another site, it was renamed Horse Shoe Baptist Church. It stood for many years until replaced by a brick church. The bell that calls worshipers to the present Horse Shoe Baptist Church is the bell from *The Mountain Lily*.

One of the two steam engines used to drive the boat's paddle wheels was taken to Transylvania County and used to run a sawmill at Island Ford Bridge near Brevard. The other engine ran a sawmill on Sugar Loaf Mountain for many years until it wore out and was junked.

For a brief moment in history, the mountaineers of Western North Carolina boasted of the highest steamship line in the world, a tribute to the enterprise of three men whose vision didn't quite match practicality on the river of snags and shoals. *The Mountain Lily* is long gone, but pork barrel remains in the mountains as well as the flatland. It is an American tradition.

A Festive Hangin' at Marshall

There is a gravestone in Patty's Chapel Cemetery with the name George Cunningham engraved upon it, a monument to one of the great mystery stories of all time in the mountains. Patty's Chapel, named for an early Methodist preacher and first pastor of the chapel, was one of the landmark Methodist churches in the mountains for the people of Cane Creek, Fletcher, and Hoopers Creek in Henderson County, south of Asheville. The cemetery, established September 11, 1855, is still maintained and used by families associated with Patty's Chapel. Located a mile off Howard Gap Road on a dirt road, it played an unwitting role in the legend of George Cunningham.

George Cunningham, born January 16, 1855, to Captain Solomon and Sarah Sophronia Fletcher Cunningham—a pioneer family in Henderson County whose descendants still live in the area, was a popular lad who began freighting when he was sixteen years old for the family store in Fletcher. George grew up rapidly, for his father, the captain, was killed in the War Between the States while serving as a Confederate officer. He, too, is buried in Patty's Chapel Cemetery.

Freighting in the 1870s in Western North Carolina was the way manufactured goods were brought into the region from the outland and farm goods moved from the Blue Ridge highlands to the lowlands of South Carolina. The two main wagon roads were north-south and east-west through the tiny village of Asheville. The north-south road was called the Buncombe Turnpike because it passed through Buncombe County on the route between Greeneville, Tennessee, and Greenville, South Carolina. The old Buncombe Turnpike went through the village of Hendersonville and the hamlet of Flat Rock before entering what is now known as the Greenville Watershed. The east-west road snaked up the Blue Ridge escarpment from Old Fort to Ridgecrest and then wandered westward through Swannanoa to Asheville and the onetime Cherokee lands surrounding the Smokies.

The wagon roads of the 1870s were little more than Cherokee Indian trails enlarged to accommodate wagons and stage coaches. Freighting in the 1870s may be compared to trucking today, only instead of wagon roads, today's freighters drive their eighteen-wheel rigs at great speeds along four-lane concrete interstate highways such as I-40 and I-26.

George Cunningham made the long hauls to and from Old Fort, down the Blue Ridge east of Asheville. He often carried rye, wheat, corn, and other farm products in his wagon for trade. On the return trip he hauled manufactured goods for the country stores that dotted the landscape at country crossroads like Hoopers Creek (Good Luck Store in Upper Hoopers Creek is an example), Cane Creek, and what is now the community of Fletcher, where the family had a store and farms. The freight wagons were pulled by four to eight mules or horses and sometimes by several yoke of oxen. The work was hard. Trips often took several days, depending on the weather and road conditions. Traders living in the present Cherokee area often took a month to complete a trip to the nearest railroad at Walhalla, South Carolina. Danger was present on the roads which were carved out of mountainsides with walls on one side and fearsome drops on the other. One misstep by teams or oxen and wagons tumbled to the bottom of gorges, coves, and hollows.

Where as today's freight haulers make stops at rest areas along the interstates, in George Cunningham's day the freighters pulled into campgrounds along roads and trails to spend the night. Late in the afternoon of June 6, 1874, George Cunningham directed his wagon team of mules into a campground near the small village of Swannanoa on the river of the same name in eastern Buncombe County. He was a two-day haul out of Old Fort en route to Cane Creek in Henderson County. His sweating mules were caked with mud from the trip as he pulled into the campground. He fed, watered, and rubbed down the mules before walking to a campfire tended by a lone rider. The stranger introduced himself as Daniel Sternberg of Kansas.

They talked a while, and then Sternberg went to his saddlebags for a pack of cards and jug of corn whiskey. They shared the contents of the jug. Then Sternberg suggested a friendly game of cards. Cunningham agreed. As the game progressed, George "Bud" Cunningham began to win. Soon he had not only Sternberg's money but also his gold watch. What happened next is gleaned from the public records of the court in Madison County and newspaper accounts of the trial of one George Cunningham of Henderson County for the murder of one Daniel Sternberg of the state of Kansas on June 6, 1874, in the county of Buncombe, state of North Carolina.

The trial, in 1875, came after the high sheriff of Buncombe County arrested George Cunningham on June 7, 1874, on "information and belief" that he had murdered Sternberg with the motive of robbery. The sheriff held out as evidence the fact that Cunningham had Sternberg's gold watch when arrested while driving his team toward the Buncombe Turnpike.

While admitting there were no witnesses to the killing of Daniel Sternberg, the sheriff said he had a confession. How the sheriff put a twist on the word confession came out in the trial. But for the moment, George Cunningham was in Buncombe County jail charged with murder.

When word reached Fletcher, Hoopers Creek, and Cane Creek that George Cunningham was in jail, there was an uproar. Cunningham was a popular young man in Henderson County, as well as being related to the most powerful family in the area, the Fletchers. Talk began that his friends planned to go to Asheville, storm the jail, and free the young man. The Buncombe County sheriff heard the talk, so he immediately moved Cunningham to the Madison County jail at Marshall to forestall any attempts at freedom.

After several delays, the trial was conducted in Marshall in June 1875. During testimony on the confession, Cunningham told the sheriff (as recorded in newspaper accounts of the time):

> I won all his money and then his watch. Sternberg grabbed the money off the ground and said mean-like to me "youse a cheat!" That made me good and mad. I picked up an axe and told him "nobody calls me a cheat and gets away with it! Put that money back down there." Sternberg leaned over and put it down, and when he did he grabbed a split rail laying by and swung it at me but hit the axe I had holdin'. He then grabbed for the axe and tried to wrestle it out of my hands. I hit him in the head with it and it killed him.

Cunningham further told the jury under questioning that as soon as he realized he had killed Sternberg, he was overcome with a sickening fear and became panicky because he knew there were no witnesses, and it would be hard to make people believe he had done it in self-defense. So he threw the man's body in the river, hitched his mules to the wagon, and started for home in Fletcher.

The trial didn't take long. The jury quickly reached a verdict of first-degree murder. The judge just as quickly sentenced Cunningham to be "hanged from the neck until dead." This was to take place on June 9, 1875. In the meantime, Dr. George Washington Fletcher and his wife, the former Elizabeth Ann Clayton, offered to pay the court Cunningham's weight in gold if the judge would release him. A graduate of the Medical College of Charleston and veteran of the Civil War as a medical officer and surgeon, Dr. Fletcher was a descendant of the family that founded Fletcher. When George Cunningham's father was killed in the Civil War, Dr. Fletcher undertook with his wife the partial rearing of the youngster.

A man's weight in gold, even for those days, was a pretty good ransom. However, neither the sheriff nor court was interested in the novel payment for a wrongful death. The hanging, the court said, would take place on the predetermined date in Marshall. At that point, Dr. Fletcher said the least he could do was pay for the construction of the scaffold upon which his nephew was to die. The sheriff and court agreed since it would save money for the county and state to have a private individual build the gallows. It was done. Dr. Fletcher's workmen set up the platform, fence, and scaffolding, along with gallows, behind the jail and courthouse in Marshall.

In 1875, roads in Madison County were little more than trails. The mountain people of the era traveled very little. Many never left their home fields because travel to the county seat of Marshall usually took one day by horseback. Entertainment such as a hanging didn't come along very often. As far as residents of the county were concerned, the hanging would be the event of the year in Madison County and perhaps the entire region of Western North Carolina. Because of the distance, residents began the trip the night before so they would be on hand in front of the courthouse by noon the next day for the great event. They came from the hills and valleys and by noon June 9, 1875, the town square in front of the Madison County Courthouse was crowded with people. It was the largest crowd in Marshall's history. It was a festive crowd, according to accounts. Then, as time for the hanging drew near, the people became quiet.

Finally the moment came when George Cunningham was led out of the jail, shackled by chains, and flanked by the sheriff and a deputy. Cunningham, now a few months past his twentieth birthday, held his head high as he surveyed the hushed crowd on his walk to the gallows. A newspaper account of the day reported:

> George Cunningham made a farewell address to approximately fifteen hundred people in which he denied to the very last he had deliberately killed Sternberg. He warned the people of the evils that could result from drinking and gambling. After this he was taken to a twenty-by-thirty-foot pen located behind the jail. The pen was surrounded by a board fence fifteen feet high. He died without a struggle.

Those within and outside the fence said that when the trap was sprung, George Cunningham fell. A doctor called, "He's dead! Cut him down." The body was immediately placed in a coffin and loaded onto a wagon. It is said that the driver of the wagon lashed the team and drove through the crowd at a rapid pace on the road to Asheville from Marshall. In those days there was no embalming, so haste was considered necessary. It was reported that one or two days later the wagon reached Fletcher, where family and friends gathered in Patty's Chapel Cemetery for the funeral and burial.

It was universal custom in the mountains in those days to open a coffin for a last view of the dead person before the burial, but this case was an exception. Because of the time that had elapsed between the hanging and burial, as well as the hot weather, it was thought best not to open the coffin of the dead man before it was lowered into the grave. This was the answer given by male members of the Cunningham and Fletcher families when asked about the viewing. A headstone listing George Cunningham's birth and death was placed at the head of the grave.

The funeral was hardly over before rumors began to spread throughout Western North Carolina that Cunningham had not been hanged until dead. The rumors were fueled by a group of men who followed the wagon and saw it pull into a wooded area, stop, and the lid of the coffin open. They rode back to Marshall and reported seeing a man get out of the coffin, jump down from the wagon, and run into the woods. A log was put into the coffin, they said. It was dusk when this happened, so it was difficult to see who the man was. The story persisted throughout the years, but nobody could say for sure what happened.

Every year or so the rumor gained new life with stories of the ghost of George Cunningham being seen on some of the back roads and trails of Henderson County. The rumors persisted even as late as 1959. Finally, family members decided it was time to find out if George Cunningham was actually buried in Patty's Chapel Cemetery. They elected a committee to have the body exhumed. Dr. David Pierce, professor of chemistry at Asheville-Biltmore College (now the University of North Carolina at Asheville), was designated by the court to open the grave at Patty's Chapel and see whether a man had been buried under the headstone of one George Cunningham in 1875.

On July 7, 1959, some eighty-four years later, the committee opened the grave at Patty's Chapel and Dr. Pierce began his examination. No remains of bones, teeth, hair, or anything resembling these things were found. The handles of the coffin were still attached to wooden portions of the casket, which were disintegrating. Dr. Pierce said the wood to which they were attached was pine. The nails from the coffin were iron and the six coffin handles were made of zinc. The cloth found in the grave was the lining of the coffin, and it was later examined in a laboratory and found to be made of lamb's wool. A considerable amount of oak wood covered with thick bark, much of it still well preserved, was also found. The only other item in the grave was a molded glass bottle on which was the inscription: "Hoyt's German Cologne, E. W. Hoyt and Co., Lowell, Massachusetts."

The oak log proved the rumor true about a log being substituted for the body of George Cunningham. Considerable discussion was held about the perfume. Walter Fletcher, then eighty-three years old, first cousin of George Cunningham, spoke up: "Years ago before embalming fluid was used in our mountains, people frequently dashed perfume on the corpse to drown out any odor of decaying flesh. It would be my supposition that if a log was buried instead of a man, someone made certain that the faked funeral was not only made to look natural but to smell natural as well."

Despite the years and proof of the opened grave, wrote Frank L. FitzSimons, famed storyteller and author of Henderson County, the mystery of the hanging of George Cunningham has become legend and will be told and retold as long as there are people in our Blue Ridge Mountains.

What really happened? Over the years bits and pieces of the story have come out. Witnesses to the hanging who were members of the family admitted many, many years later that the scaffolding built by Dr. Fletcher was designed so that when the trap was sprung George Cunningham's feet would touch the ground and the rope would not break his neck. The doctor, family member Pres Johnson and others admit, was none other than Dr. Fletcher, George Cunningham's uncle. He shouted the order to cut him down so the young man would not be injured after the fall. Johnson also told Frank FitzSimons about the oak log used to make it seem as though a body was in the coffin when the pallbearers carried it to the grave for burial. The men who followed the wagon with the coffin did see Cunningham jump out and run into the woods. Old-timers said they did see George Cunningham on the back roads of Fletcher from time to time as he moved under cover of darkness to visit his beloved mother. But family members didn't really know the whole story because Dr. Fletcher and others who conspired to help Cunningham beat the gallows said nothing about the rumors or the hanging over their lifetimes. They rode out the storm of rumor in silence.

The opening of the grave in 1959 proved George Cunningham is not buried in that grave. The role Dr. Fletcher played indicated that while the hanging had, in effect, fulfilled the sentence of the court, it had, in reality, not.

When the court did not accept Dr. Fletcher's offer of ransom, the good doctor took another tack. He figured out a way to have his nephew hang and live at the same time. Often in that era, mountain folks took matters into their own hands if they thought the courts had erred or that a jury had not returned a fair verdict. That happened here. But what of George Cunningham? What happened to him?

It wasn't until 1986 that a family member confirmed a pattern of behavior so common in the mountain in the 1850s through the 1880s. It is called GTT. Many abandoned cabins had GTT carved in their doors to tell those who followed what had happened to the original occupants of the cabin. You see, GTT means "Gone To Texas" in the shorthand of the mountains. When men or women found trouble in the mountains, they picked up their belongings and rode into the sunset toward Texas. A good living could be had as a cowboy or freighter or mule skinner in the West if one kept his mouth shut and said nothing. It also was considered uncouth to ask a stranger where he came from or his business back home. If a person did his work, kept still, and stayed out of trouble, no one asked why he was in Texas or the Indian Territory.

In 1986, this writer presented the GTT theory to a member of the Cunningham family and the surprising answer was: "You guessed it." George Cunningham did go to Texas. He did make trips back home to see his mother. How do we know? His brother, Preston Brooks Cunningham, told his son many, many years later before he died. His son then told his daughter before he died, and the daughter confirmed it when asked.

Preston Cunningham made several trips away from Fletcher for weeks at a time during his lifetime. He told members of the family he had to travel by train, but they were never to ask him where or why he went. Family members considered the mystery trips a dark secret for years. In later years, one member of the family said, the women talked about the hanging that wasn't, and considered the escape of George Cunningham to be a great story. However, men in the family still would not talk about the event, or when they did talk, it was only in small groups where nobody could listen in.

Yes, Preston Cunningham visited his brother George in Texas as long as he lived. Yes, George Cunningham came back to the mountains on occasion. Where George Cunningham lived in Texas is not known or whether he used his given name. However, family members say he married and had a family. It is known that he never got into any trouble and became a solid citizen of Texas. A rumor that persists to this day is that his body was brought back to Patty's Chapel Cemetery when he died of old age in Texas, and that there are two graves marked George Cunningham in the cemetery. Today, there is only one with his name on it.

If George Cunningham had lived to seventy years of age, he would have died sometime in 1925. Somewhere in Texas, it is believed, there is another Cunningham family related to the one in Western North Carolina. Someday the rest of the story may be told.

Blockade and Blockaders

One of the stereotypes of the Blue Ridge and Great Smoky Mountains is of the wily moonshiner. Comic strips, books, movies, and television often portray the old-time moonshiner as a fellow in bib overalls, tall black felt hat, gun cradled in his arms, with a jug of spirits corked with a corncob. Stereotypes die hard, perhaps because the stereotype of the mountain moonshiner from 1860 through the 1930s did contain an element of truth coupled with a fictional mythical glamour which made it difficult to distinguish fact from fiction.

Mountaineers did dress in bib overalls and tall black felt hats sometimes. When in the forest or field they did carry a gun cradled in their arms, better to have a gun handy in case one saw a rabbit, squirrel, deer, wild boar, or bear, all necessary for food. But moonshiners of the era often wore wool trousers and shirts, wool hats, black suits, canvas trousers, and boots. Moonshiners came from all walks of life, ranging from those who made products, operated stores, farmed, and even preached. Some moonshiners made liquor for home use, while others made it to sell. Writers of the era and later used the stereotype as folklore in and out of the mountains in remembrance of a day now long gone and, once in a while, not so long gone.

Occasionally an illegal still is found by law enforcement officers in the mountains of eastern Tennessee and Western North Carolina, but there are better cash crops now than moonshine.

Moonshine is the name given to corn whiskey made in a small family still in a mountain hollow, poured into pint- or quart-sized glass jars, and sold in the big cities of the North and South, to regular customers or used for home consumption. Before glass jars, the earthenware jug was the usual container. Since cork was scarce in the mountains, the traditional corn cob was used to cap the jugs containing mountain corn whiskey.

No excise taxes were paid, thus making the whiskey and its sale illegal according to state and federal laws. Perhaps this is where the myth and glamour came in. Anything secretive is bound to attract attention and moonshining is no exception. The more secretive, the more glamorous.

People from outside the mountains were known in the past as *outlanders*, the English word for *sassenach,* as foreigners were called in Scotland since at least the fifteenth century. These outsiders referred to corn whiskey as *moonshine*, but in the mountains it is known as *blockade* and its makers as *blockaders*. The *moonshine* tab probably came about because English smugglers of brandy from Holland in the 1700s were called *moonlighters*. Old-timers in the mountains, not knowing about brandy smugglers, attribute the names *moonshine* and *moonshiners* to the fact that blockaders often fired up their stills at night by the light of the moon. Darkness would cover smoke from the still, and a full or even a three-quarter moon provided enough light to work by without resorting to lantern light, something that could be seen for miles around in the mountains at night. The product would be *moonshine*. The *blockade* name is a result of government agents attempting to halt the flow of illegal liquor by setting up road blocks or blockades on routes used to transport whiskey. Often these blockades would be at the entrances of coves and hollows.

The making of blockade as a cottage industry in the mountains of eastern Tennessee and Western North Carolina really goes back to Scotland and Ireland for it was the immigrant Scots from the Highlands and the Scots-Irish from Northern Ireland who brought to the United States the skill of whiskey making learned in their native lands. The Scots, of course, learned whiskey making in the Highlands where even today the finest Scotch whiskey in the world is made. What makes Scotch so good, according to connoisseurs, is the peat burned to dry the grains used in the making of the whiskeys which are blended to make the Scotch. Ireland's contribution is Irish whiskey produced in small pot (*poteen*) distilleries ("stills"). Irish whiskey is not blended as with Scotch. The Scots-Irish left Northern Ireland because, among other reasons, the English placed excise taxes on their whiskey.

Gateway to the New World for the Scots-Irish was Philadelphia. The natural westward migration led the Scots-Irish into middle and western Pennsylvania where *Deutsche* or Pennsylvania Dutch (German) immigrants had settled and developed beautiful farms. However, that region soon became crowded, so the immigrants moved south along the Shenandoah Valley and to the Piedmont of North Carolina. When the former Cherokee lands opened up in Western North Carolina and eastern Tennessee after the Revolutionary War, the Scots-Irish and German families seeking new land and homes moved into the mountains, a place similar to the Highlands of Scotland and the Connemara region of Ireland. The new settlers brought with them the ability and skills to make whiskey in small, family poteen stills.

Some people call the corn whiskey of the mountains the *elixir* or *water of life* while others call it *popskull.*

The *elixir* name probably came about when whiskey was considered a medicine in an era when doctors and pharmacies were few and far between. Besides herbs, or *yarbs* as the mountain people called them, there was a number of elixirs or patented medicines on the market between 1860 and 1940 that had alcohol as their base. Whiskey in any form was considered good for chills, spills, snakebite, and general malaise. Alcohol was an important ingredient in the production of medicines in the blockade era, and it could be made at home with materials at hand. Do-it-yourself medicine was a mountain way. Thus, whiskey played a major role in the home. If an old-timer wanted to entertain a guest at his cabin or camp, he'd call upon a member of the family to "fetch the elixir." Corn liquor is what the head of the household asked for and received. It often was retrieved from under the floor of the corn crib, considered a safe place.

Blockade was called *popskull* by the lumberjacks who cut down the great Appalachian forests from 1900 to 1930. That was because corn liquor is usually fresh (not aged more than a day or two), high proof (high alcohol content), and so direct (it hits with force) it leaves the impression that a drinker's skull is about to pop. Corn whiskey's directness also led to its being called *white lightning* by some of its drinkers. Even today that is a name some people give it, usually in the big city slums and red clay country of some southern states.

The word *pizen* came into use after automobiles came on the market. Old automobile radiators made ideal *cooling worms,* a term referring to any winding radiator-type line used to cool the liquid product. The auto radiators worked perfectly, except for one nasty fact of life: They are put together with lead, and lead salts are poisonous. Many blockaders or moonshiners found out too late that the liquor they were making had a tendency to create lead poisoning when imbibed, which in turn led to one's death. However, the good and true mountain whiskey maker used copper stills and no lead soldering. You could still get a headache from copper-still corn whiskey. It might be popskull, but it wasn't pizen.

The making of corn liquor in the mountains is intertwined with government, the collection of taxes, commerce, and the need for good transportation systems to carry products from farm to market. It also is tied to the formation of two different political philosophies which developed into the Federalist and Republican (later the Democratic) parties.

During President George Washington's first term in office, he went outside the Constitution and organized a Cabinet to advise him on economic and foreign affairs. He appointed Alexander Hamilton, author of the *Federalist Papers*, as secretary of the Treasury. Hamilton believed in a strong central government as opposed to Thomas Jefferson, a later president, who advocated a weak central government with the states having more power. Today's states' rights debates began way back then. Jefferson, who was Washington's secretary of state, opposed subsidies, tariffs, and the capitalistic ideas of Hamilton and John Adams. In those days a person who advocated a democratic style of government was called a Republican while those who favored a less democratic style of government a Federalist.

Hamilton thought that finance and manufacturing had to be encouraged, so he advocated the new Federal government's assumption of $50 million in Revolutionary War debt and $20 million in debt incurred by the states in the war. He proposed to finance the debt by issuing bonds. Now, what did all of this have to do with whiskey? Hamilton proposed that the $70 million debt be financed with an excise tax on whiskey. He also had in mind an increase in the government's power to tax and to demonstrate that power to the very independent whiskey makers in western Pennsylvania, many of whom learned their trade in Scotland and Ireland before emigrating to the colonies.

The whiskey makers considered the tax a blow to their income, because roads were so poor the only way many farmers could get grain to market was to reduce its bulk into whiskey. This is the same situation that led to moonshining in the mountains at a later date. Discontent in the back country of Pennsylvania led to riots and the tarring and feathering of federal tax agents in 1794. President Washington had a crisis on his hands. He called the state militias to active duty in order to put down the rebellion, thus a testing the principle of Presidential control over federal law enforcement, including the right to command the use of state militia troops. The Whiskey Rebellion of western Pennsylvania was put down. The tax background is necessary to understand the reason, to a great degree, moonshining became an industry in the mountains and why mountain people relished isolation and no taxes.

The War of 1812 resulted in the next excise tax on whiskey. This was lifted in 1817. It wasn't until 1862 that another excise tax was placed on whiskey. This time a $.20-a-gallon tax was levied to help finance the Civil War by the federal government. It went to $1.50 a gallon in 1864 and the following year jumped to $2.00 a gallon. In 1868, the tax went back to $.50 a gallon but then jumped to $.70 in 1872 and $.90 in 1875. The rise in the tax in 1875 resulted in a dramatic increase in the number of illegal stills in the back country of Western North Carolina and eastern Tennessee. The use of excise taxes through the turn of the century and well into the 1960s would continue to be a source of irritation to residents in the mountains.

Moonshining increased in 1919, right after World War I, when national Prohibition was proclaimed. Illegal liquor became a valuable commodity during that national experiment, which was in force for a little over a decade.

Another key factor in the number of stills, mentioned before, was the lack of good transportation in the mountains. It is difficult for modern-day Americans to realize the difficulty and near impossibility of travel in the Appalachian Mountains before 1920. What began as buffalo trails evolved into Indian foot trails, horse trails, and finally into wagon roads. Old-timers emphasize time and again the hardship of not having a good wagon road until the late 1890s, and then little travel with wagons could be done because even the rude wagon roads were often strewn with boulders, followed stream beds in places, and often hugged mountain sides with such a narrow track that wagon driver and horses risked a fall anytime they tried passage. Residents of Crossnore near Linville didn't see a good wagon road until around 1916, and then it wasn't until the 1920s that North Carolina began a drive to have what the public and politicians called the major issue of the day: "Good Roads." It wasn't until the 1930s that paving was started on many main mountain roads in the state.

Thus, trails made up the route taken through most areas in the mountains for a very long time. The trails crisscrossed the steep-sided hollows and ridges. Even today it is possible to follow old trails and wagon roads from one place to another without traveling on the paved roads. The poor roads and trails prevented mountain families from transporting their cash crop—corn—to market. The settlers discovered that they could distill the corn into whiskey, and that could be more easily transported by yoked oxen or horseback to the county seat or hamlet store where it would fetch cash.

Corn used for food was usually taken in a tote bag to the nearest grist mill; or, if no grist mill was nearby, it was taken to the nearest tub mill, where it sometimes would take all day to grind a couple of pounds of cornmeal. The meal was used to make bread, a staple of diet along with bear meat, beef, and venison cured and hung in the smokehouse.

Thus, corn whiskey was a cash crop with proceeds from its sale used to obtain salt, baking soda, and other products the mountain people could not raise or make themselves. To tax whiskey, they reasoned, was a direct attack on their livelihood and they resisted.

As railroads branched out along the valleys, logging camps sprouted at the base of mountains and in coves near the railheads, and when a person could travel by train to Asheville or Knoxville, the market for whiskey expanded.

There is a third reason mountain people often produced moonshine from time to time, and that had to do with prices paid for farm products. Periodically farmers, especially those small farmers in Western North Carolina and eastern Tennessee, faced financial disaster when the selling price of their agricultural products dropped below their investment expenses, and no money meant ruin. At those times, the small farmers turned to moonshining to carry them over to better times. Revenue agents were sent back into the hills to find stills, but the isolation worked in favor of the mountain people, as did another interesting aspect of life—the suspension from time to time by mutual consent of Federal law and regulations. This came about in an unusual way and became, in some instances, tradition. The only representative of the Federal government that most mountain people ever knew was the crossroads postmaster. He usually was the storekeeper too. He also could read and write. While a representative of the "g'verment," he also was a friend and neighbor with whom everyone did business. Because the pay was low, the postmaster, like everybody else, had to hunt and fish on a regular basis to put food on the table. If the postmaster was away on one of his periodic hunting or fishing trips, it was not unusual for residents to walk into the store-post office, collect their mail, issue stamps to themselves, and conduct other business. This casual approach was called "suspension of the regulations by mutual consent."

If postal regulations could be suspended by mutual consent, so could other regulations and laws if such was necessary for survival in the rugged mountains. The reasoning was thus: If you couldn't carry ten bushels of corn to Asheville, Greenville, Spartanburg, Newport, or Knoxville on your back over nonexistent roads to market in order to get cash to survive, you could carry the same ten bushels in liquid form and get cash that way. It made sense to suspend the rules and laws that forbade the making and transporting of corn whiskey. The battle between blockader and revenuer, the wets and drys, church people and others, country people and those citified, raged for years in Western North Carolina and eastern Tennessee.

One of the oft-repeated stories in the mountains is about the good ole' boys in early stock car racing in this country and how they learned to drive on the mountain roads of Western North Carolina and eastern Tennessee while hauling blockade whiskey to market. There is a grain of truth to the story.

Blockaders always nestled their stills near a branch (mountain stream) because good, cool water is necessary to making good blockade whiskey. The blockaders also placed their stills away from the view of passers by. They always had an escape route in the event a revenuer or group of agents came near. Blockaders also tried to choose a place where anyone coming near could be spotted long before arrival. To keep from creating a still path, the blockaders would approach and leave the still area via a different direction each time. A path into a thicket near water often indicated a still nearby. In fact, when agents are searching for a still in a hollow, the first sign they look for is the still path. Revenue agents also learned early that horses will not drink from a branch or stream polluted with sour mash or alcohol. Many a still has been accidentally located when an agent reached a stream and his horse refused to drink the water. A search upstream would usually reveal an operating still.

Sometimes agents would not search for an operating still right away when they discovered a still path or polluted stream but, instead, would stake it out over a period of time to discover who was making blockade and how they were going about it. It was important to catch the blockaders.

A major problem in the making of blockade liquor was the grinding of sprouted corn. In earlier days grinding sprouted corn was no less an offense against the law of the United States than was actually making whiskey. Thus, a blockader had to get a couple of bushels of sprouted corn to a mill and back without the neighbors becoming suspicious, and a miller had to agree to take the risk. The problem was often easily solved because nearly every third or fourth farm in the mountains had a primitive tub mill. These little mills could turn out a bushel of milled corn in a day. In Ireland, the distillers learned to turn the starch of the grain into sugar with malt;

but in the mountains where they emigrated, malt was difficult to come by, so they would place the unground corn in a container with a hole at the bottom and top. Hot water was percolated through the container for the number of days it took to sprout the corn. Then the corn was dried and ground.

Modern-day moonshiners use sugar purchased wholesale to help grain ferment. And just as often the wholesalers—and even retailers—will tip off agents if too much sugar is purchased by one person. In the old-fashioned way, the ground cornmeal was made into a mash with boiling water. This was allowed to stand for eight to ten days as it fermented. If malt or yeast was added it would ferment rapidly, but most mountain men had to wait and watch their mash. Since blockaders did not have sophisticated equipment, they went by intuition and experience in determining when mash had turned to sour mash or *beer*.

The beer was placed in the still, a container with a closed head and spiral tube running throughout. Cold water drawn by pipe or line from a stream would circulate inside the container. A wood fire would be built under the still, and the alcohol would rise as vapor from the cooking sour mash and then condense in the cold worm and trickle down into what blockaders called the *receiver*.

Blockaders usually built their fires in a firebox at night so the smoke could not be seen, and the smell would blend into the smoke from cabin fireplaces where the cooking and heating was done. They worked by night and the light of the moon.

Because the old-time mountain blockaders had to depend on skill based on experience rather than sophisticated equipment, the ability of certain mountain men to make good whiskey was cherished. Too short a distillation meant poor or rank alcohol; too long meant pure alcohol. The blockaders tested the product until it showed a *bead* or small bubbles in the drink. If the bubbles or bead rise is persistent, it is good whiskey; if not—bad stuff.

Blockaders called the first spirits *singlings* because they were the result of a single distillation. When run through the worm a second time, the result would be *doublings*. Normally blockaders did not run doublings. But to ensure good whiskey with singlings, they used a thump chest. This was actually a steam chest or barrel that thumped loudly when the liquor went through. Its advantage: It allowed the blockaders to make their whiskey smoother faster, before the revenue agents caught wind of the still. A final touch was to run the whiskey through a rude charcoal filter to get rid of the fusel oil, an oily, acidic poison that develops naturally during the distillation process. Blockade whiskey was then ready to drink. Of course, some folks would age it—a day or so.

Professional distillers like the people at Lynchburg, Tennessee, where Jack Daniels opened the first licensed distillery, or George Dickel Distillery in nearby Tullahoma, use much the same process only on a larger quantity basis to produce what whiskey lovers call "sippin' whiskey." The difference, they say, is in the ingredients, water, charcoal, and aging process. Bourbon whiskey, first made in Bourbon County, Kentucky, has less rye and barley than Tennessee whiskey. Kentucky Bourbon, it should be noted, was first made by a minister in Bourbon County.

Originally transport of blockade whiskey in the mountains was by jug. In later years it was usually put into pint or quart glass jars of the style used for home canning, since most homes had them. Little has changed over the years, and even into the 1960s there were stills in the mountains. In fact, Cocke County, Tennessee, reportedly had more than two hundred stills running around the clock in the 1960s, furnishing corn liquor to major cities. The cottage industry had grown to a $13-million-a-year illegal business. The growth in 1960 was due to the federal government's $10.50 a gallon tax on bonded whiskey. The stills in Cocke County cost the federal government $37,000 a day in lost taxes, meanwhile increasing the profits of everybody in the moonshining chain.

Of course, commercial moonshining is a different business than the one operated by individual mountaineers. For example, where the old-fashioned moonshiner ground a few pounds of corn for his still, the modern-day professional uses a recipe that requires seventy-five pounds of white cornmeal, three hundred pounds of sugar, one pound of yeast, fifteen pounds of bran, and three hundred gallons of water for a yield of forty-eight gallons of moonshine every four days. By changing the recipe, a moonshiner may increase the yield to any amount as long as the still can produce it.

The following newspaper story appeared in the Hendersonville *Times-News* in 1966. It easily could have appeared in the *Asheville*

Citizen-Times or half dozen weekly newspapers serving Western North Carolina and eastern Tennessee. (The identity of the single subject in this story remains concealed.)

HENDERSONVILLE - Who says the good old days are gone forever?

You can't prove it by Alcohol Beverage Control officers in Polk, Henderson and Buncombe counties.

They raided an old fashioned moonshine still in the wilds of Polk County shortly before noon Monday which turned out to be one of the biggest mountain whiskey operations uncovered in recent years.

"It was a classic operation," said Jim Bartlett, veteran Henderson County ABC enforcement officer. "It had everything including a lookout."

Abe Lynch, Polk Country ABC enforcement officer, led the raid in which Bartlett, A. A. Dowtin, chief of enforcement in Asheville, and Charles Giglia, enforcement officer in Asheville, also took part.

Lynch and Bartlett sensed something was going on about two weeks ago when moonshine began showing up in Henderson County.

The white lightning, deadly poison because of lead salts from an automobile radiator condenser, was selling for $10-a-gallon on the bootleg market.

Word on the "grapevine" had the illegal still in operation somewhere on Hogback Mountain, deep in the Blue Ridge near the North Carolina-South Carolina state line.

Lynch and Bartlett called the Asheville men and the four began their search for the still yesterday morning.

By Jeep and truck they left Tryon and headed for Hogback, a wilderness that runs from Polk across Henderson toward Transylvania County.

The area has been a favorite of blockaders since the turn of the century.

Lynch and Bartlett parked their Jeep at the head of an old logging trail on Hogback and started on foot in search of a "still" path.

As they walked down the road, they were spotted by a lookout for the still who was crouched in a nearby laurel thicket.

After they passed, the lookout followed the two revenoors down the road.

"I thought they were some Yankees lookin' at some land to buy but when I saw them guns I knew they was revenoors," said _____, a sixty-two-year-old mountaineer who lives atop Hogback.

Unknown to_____, who was cited to appear in court in Tryon today for a hearing on being the lookout, he was being followed by one of the Asheville agents.

When ______ saw the agents ahead of him stop at the still path, he sounded the alarm.

"Fire in the hole, fire in the hole," he shouted, "fire in the hole."

Lynch and Giglia chased ______, who started running through a thicket while Bartlett, who spied the still down the mountain, went crashing through the underbrush in an attempt to head off the men working at the still site.

Bartlett sliced through the trees like a bulldozer gone wild while the two men at the still raced down the cove and into the trackless laurel and rhododendron. Fire was blowing out the top of that one-hundred-gallon upright boiler still and everything was hissin' and chuggin'," said Bartlett.

They got away. The agent, accompanied by ______ went back to the site of the still.

"Fire was blowing out the top of that 100 gallon upright boiler and everything was hissin' and chuggin'," said Bartlett.

The blockaders were half done in their day's work. Sixty gallons of moonshine whiskey was stacked near the top of the still path to await the truck that would take it down the mountain at nightfall.

"Half of the twenty fifty-five gallon drums were filled with sour mash," Lynch pointed out.

The still could turn out 120-gallons of whiskey a day.

The cooling condenser was a truck radiator immersed in a tank of water. The white liquor ran by gravity to another steel tank where gallon jugs were filled.

The whole operation was perched on the sheer side of a laurel thicket.

Water for the operation was piped via rubber hose from a stream up the mountain.

The fire was from an oil burner fed from a fifty-gallon oil tank wedged against a tree. Oil was brought to the site in five. gallon cans. Off to the side were two hundred-pound bags of sugar.

The men at the still had scooted off without a fried chicken lunch that had been prepared for them.

Old ______, the lookout, sat down as the agents began

the task of fixing the dynamite to blow up the still. He told the agents he wasn't going anyplace.

"My word's my honor," he said.

"This still has been working three months," one of the agents said.

"Six weeks," interrupted ______.

"Who was runnin' it?" asked Bartlett.

"Now fellows," said ______, "if somebody gave you $15-a-day to yell 'fire in the hole' would you tell on them?"

"I had nothing to do with it. I jist set up thar and kept watch." The agents admitted they didn't have much of a case against ______. Aiding and abetting would be the charge, if they could prove it. "You've got to catch them at the still," said one agent, "to prove it."

Suddenly the mountain turned dark and the rain came.

The agents put the dynamite amid the fermenting mash, steel column, and snake-like water and liquor lines and lit the fuse. A minute later a series of explosions rent the air.

Shrapnel and sour mash flew skyward as a white cloud of steam and smoke drifted across Hogback Mountain.

"Yes," admitted the old man, "thar was a real still."

The Tale of Abraham Lincoln's Birth

In the Blue Ridge and Great Smoky Mountains, tradition and family versions of history often carry more weight than official versions of the same history.

Pioneer days in the Smokies had their own secrets. One of them is that President Abraham Lincoln was born in Western North Carolina's mountains, not in Kentucky on February 12, 1809, as listed on the official record and accepted by historians around the world. The oral tradition is also in dispute over the identity of his father. Was it Thomas Lincoln or another man? And which Nancy Hanks among a dozen or so having the same name was his mother?

While the story of Lincoln's North Carolina origin is not accepted by historians as true, it is a twice-told tale in the Blue Ridge and Great Smokies. For that reason it is included among the tales told and retold in the mountains. It is said in the coves, ridges, bottom lands, and hamlets that everybody in the mountains is related either by blood, marriage, or affair. This is true enough to bring chuckles from those who share the secrets of family in the mountains.

Two unofficial biographies of Lincoln—one by his law partner in Springfield, Illinois—were suppressed by Lincoln supporters when they were published after his assassination in 1865. Attorney William Herndon, Lincoln's law partner, speculates the biographies were squelched because both listed Lincoln as the illegitimate son of Nancy Hanks. For the eighteenth president of the United States—called the greatest president since George Washington—illegitimacy was a bit much for the nation's elite when there was great emphasis on lineage on the part of the governing aristocracy.

The highest compliment in the 1870s and '80s was that a person was born of *good stock*. Being born out of wedlock then meant you were not of good stock. Those who knew Lincoln well said he carried a burden all his life, and they attribute his sadness and inner conflict with his secret knowledge of his parentage.

One of the major families in the Smokies is that of Abraham Enloe, a livestock trader and farmer who moved from Rutherford County, North Carolina, in the foothills of the Blue Ridge to Oconaluftee (now Cherokee and the edge of the Great Smoky Mountains National Park) in the early 1800s. There he raised livestock, traded in slaves, and farmed the land. At one time the present farmstead and museum at the entrance of the park was called the Floyd-Enloe Bottoms. Mingus Mill was owned by a brother-in-law to Abraham Enloe. In fact, Enloe is referred to as a miller in some of the versions of the story. According to the Enloe family, Abraham Lincoln was the son of Abraham Enloe by Nancy Hanks.

The Enloe story is only half of the speculation on Lincoln's father. The other half of the story involves his great rival, John C. Calhoun, the famed state's rights senator from South Carolina whose plantation, Fort Hill, is now Clemson University. The Calhoun family tradition is that a young John C. Calhoun became involved with a Nancy Hanks while he was studying law in the Pendleton District of South Carolina, and a son was born of that liaison. Both oral traditions merge with one Nancy Hanks and two powerful men, Abraham Enloe and John C. Calhoun, each considered by some to be the father of the Great Emancipator.

The separation of fact from fiction was attempted by Judge Felix Alley, a mountain man from the Whiteside section of Western North Carolina who married into the Enloe family. His book, *Random Thoughts and the Musings of a Mountaineer*, lays out the various oral traditions in legal manner to a surprising conclusion. The chapters on Lincoln also anger scholars who say there is no evidence that Judge Alley is correct in his assumptions and conclusions. Here is what Judge Alley found in his research.

Lincoln's mother, Nancy Hanks, was born the illegitimate daughter of Lucy Hanks of Amelia County, Virginia. Oral tradition names a Michael Tanner, also of Amelia County, as her father. Lincoln himself said his mother's father was an obscure Virginia planter. The Hanks family is of English background. A number of the family members migrated from Amelia County to Gaston County, North Carolina, where little Nancy Hanks traveled about the county with her mother, Lucy, and a sister Mandy, while Lucy spun flax for a living. Lucy Hanks and her children would live with the people for whom Lucy spun flax until the job was done, and then they would move on to the next family. It was a hand-to-mouth existence.

When they did live in one place it was with Lucy's brother, Dicky Hanks, in a log cabin on the bluffs above of the Catawba River near Belmont, North Carolina. Dicky Hanks was once put in jail in Rutherford and ordered to make shoes. The proceeds went to Lucy Hanks and the girls. Because he would spend all of his earnings on liquor when out of jail, county officials decided to put Dicky to work without the liquor in an effort to have him support his sister and her daughters. Lucy and the children also stayed with a "Granny" Hollifield in Rutherford County at one time, according to research by Judge Alley.

At this point Nancy's life crosses with Abraham Enloe. Both Nancy and Mandy, according to Judge Alley, were bound out to families. Mandy went with a Pratt family, and Nancy went with the Enloe family when she was about ten years of age. Both families lived in Rutherford County, North Carolina

The record shows that in 1803, Abraham Enloe sold several of his farms in Rutherford County and removed to Oconaluftee in Swain County, taking his family and little Nancy Hanks with him. The Oconaluftee River flows out of the Smokies and through the present-day Cherokee Indian Reservation. Abraham Enloe purchased and raised cattle, horses, mules, and became a merchant and trader with businessmen in Augusta, Georgia; Charleston, South Carolina; and other markets in the South. He made two trips a year with stock and returned with merchandise such as salt, sugar, coffee, and other articles for his trading post in the Smokies. He became a very prosperous businessman in the early 1800s.

By this time Nancy Hanks, who was developing into a beautiful young lady, lived in the Enloe household. She stayed there until her aunt, Ann Hanks inherited a tavern from her husband at Craytonville, South Carolina, in the Pendleton District between Abbeville and Anderson. It was in this same district that a very young John C. Calhoun was studying law. Nancy left Oconaluftee and the Enloe household and went to work for her aunt as a barmaid in the tavern at Craytonville.

For lawyers and judges on the court circuit in those days, the tavern operated by Luke Hanks' widow Ann was a common stopover. It is at Craytonville where Abraham Enloe, John C. Calhoun, and Thomas Lincoln, a drover for Enloe, all crossed paths with the now-grown Nancy Hanks, and with each other.

In his book, Judge Alley unravels the various family connections of the Hanks family with documentation and affidavits until he succeeds in placing Nancy Hanks in the Pendleton District and in contact with Calhoun, Enloe, and Thomas Lincoln at the same place during the same time. Judge Alley also found that another contemporary of Abraham Lincoln's, Judge James L. Orr, became curious about the rumors involving the tavern, Nancy Hanks, and Calhoun. When he went to Congress from the district and met Lincoln, also a congressman at that time, Judge Orr was struck by the similarity in looks between Lincoln and the Hanks family men. He spoke to Lincoln about it, and the future president remarked that his mother was Nancy Hanks. When Judge Orr pressed the future president about the rest of his ancestry, Lincoln refused to talk about the subject and walked away. This made Judge Orr even more curious, so when he returned to Anderson County, South Carolina, from Washington, he went to the Hanks family and asked about the Calhoun connection.

The Hanks family members told Judge Orr their story of Nancy Hanks' involvement with John C. Calhoun in an illicit love affair, and her subsequent removal from the district and state. They recounted that when John C. Calhoun had just begun the practice of law, he often stayed at the Craytonville tavern operated by Ann Hanks while on trips around the circuit court. When

Nancy's condition became known, the Hanks family called upon Calhoun for reparation. The two clans met at the old tavern with both Nancy and John present. They both acknowledged that the unborn child being carried by Nancy was Calhoun's child.

"Calhoun agreed to pay Nancy five hundred dollars to enable her to 'leave the country,' so that the scandal might not hurt him, with the understanding that Nancy was to have time in which to communicate with a relative then living in Tennessee to whose home she desired to go," Judge Alley wrote in his book.

Staying at the tavern at the same time was Abraham Enloe and his drover, Thomas Lincoln, who were on their way to Augusta and Charleston with livestock and slaves. Remember, Nancy Hanks had lived in the Enloe household during her teen years. To Nancy, Enloe was a father figure and Thomas Lincoln his chief hired hand. When the Calhouns found out that Enloe and Lincoln knew Nancy, and that she had lived in the Enloe household, they hired Lincoln to take Nancy home with them to Oconaluftee on their return trip, and then on to Tennessee or Kentucky. The five hundred dollars was to go to Lincoln for his efforts.

Judge Alley notes that Judge Orr was a man of great credentials who told friends in Abbeville of the Calhoun-Hanks arrangement. Judge Orr was also a congressman who later became speaker of the U.S. House of Representatives in the Thirty-fifth Congress; governor of South Carolina; and, in 1870, was named Ambassador to Russia by President U. S. Grant. Then Judge Alley turns directly to descendants of John C. Calhoun for their oral tradition and version of the story. Judge Orr was the brother-in-law of Mrs. Fannie Marshall, a second cousin of John C. Calhoun, and during conversation about the subject she admitted the truth of the story. The Calhoun family also told the facts to Dr. W. C. Brown, the brother of Joe Brown, the "War Governor" of Georgia.

The version put forth by some members of the Calhoun family places Nancy Hanks in the Calhoun household in Abbeville, working in the home when young John had lived there with his mother. The Calhoun family admitted to friends in private that John C. Calhoun had an affair with Nancy Hanks in Abbeville, whether at her aunt's tavern or in his home, and was the father of the baby she named Abraham.

Why did the Enloe clan think Abraham Enloe was the father of

Nancy Hanks' child? Mrs. Enloe was a jealous woman. Nancy Hanks lived in the Enloe household from nine or ten years of age until she matured. While she left the household to work at her aunt's tavern in Abbeville, she would have continued to see Abraham Enloe on his trips to Augusta and Charleston. Mrs. Enloe did not trust her husband for some reason. This was pointed out in affidavits garnered by Judge Alley in his research. Circumstantial evidence points to an affair between Enloe and Nancy at some time in their lives at Oconaluftee, and Mrs. Enloe tended to think the worst about her husband's trips rather than to absolve him. As Judge Alley noted, nothing but the removal of Nancy from any area where she could have contact with Abraham Enloe would satisfy Mrs. Enloe. To appease his wife, Enloe began steps to have Nancy go to Kentucky. Before that could happen, tradition says, Nancy gave birth to a baby boy somewhere in the mountains and named the child Abraham. This further inflamed Mrs. Enloe since Abraham was the name of her husband.

In the mountains a child born out of wedlock is often named after the real father. There is no evidence to this fact in this case, but Mrs. Enloe was suspicious. Abraham also was the name of Nancy Hanks' grandfather Hanks. Some say the birth took place at Oconaluftee; some say the birth was at the home of Felix Walker just north of Waynesville, or in Rutherford County where the Enloe clan lived before moving to the Smokies. There are different stories on the birthplace. The Rutherford County property where the Enloes lived before moving to Cherokee is still called Lincoln Hill. Felix Walker was a friend of Enloe and the first congressman from the Western North Carolina district.

Nancy Hanks hid herself so well during the time she was away from the Enloe home awaiting the birth of her child that no one knew where she was, where all she traveled, or whether she was even alive. Rumors spread throughout the community that she was missing, that Tom Lincoln had killed her, and that there ought to be a lynching. Felix Walker finally had Michael Tanner, Nancy's alleged father, bring her back to Oconaluftee to prove Nancy and child were indeed still alive. Rumors spread rapidly in the mountains in those days, and could often incite action.

After Nancy was back in the Enloe household with a babe in arms, Mrs. Enloe continued to be agitated. She wanted Nancy out and away from the place. Thomas Lincoln, Enloe's hired hand, had done the job the Calhouns asked of him by getting Nancy away from the Pendleton District where the situation could have embarrassed young John C. Calhoun at the start of his legal career. For his effort, Lincoln was paid $500 by the Calhoun family. Now it was Enloe's turn. He agreed to pay Thomas Lincoln another $500, a wagon, and a pair of mules if he would take Nancy completely out of North Carolina and assume paternity of her child. Family lore has Enloe's married daughter taking Nancy, Thomas, and little Abraham to some location near Elizabethton, Tennessee, before they all moved on to Kentucky. The family of Felix Walker noted in affidavit that the former congressman aided in the removal of Nancy and child from North Carolina. Oral tradition has the family stopping for a year in Tennessee before moving on to Kentucky where Nancy married Thomas Lincoln in 1806.

Thomas Lincoln, according to Lincoln biographers and historians as well as Lincoln himself, was a rather shiftless fellow who did little to support his family. One of the stories about his nature involves a vicious fight between Abraham Enloe and Thomas Lincoln when Enloe refused to pay Lincoln the $500, two mules, and wagon because Thomas did not immediately marry Nancy, assume paternity of the child, and move away. Judge Alley quotes Berry H. Melton, Enloe's nephew who witnessed the fight:

> Uncle refused to pay him the full amount, and they had trouble. Lincoln got drunk and threatened Enloe and they got into a fight. They fought just like bull dogs. Old Lincoln got uncle down and bit off the end of his nose.

Enloe carried the scar the rest of his life. Melton noted that after the fight between Lincoln and Enloe, the two again became friends and Tom Lincoln brought Nancy and little Abe to Swain County to see Enloe. The real reason for the visit was Tom Lincoln needed the mare and mule and a little pocket change for taking care of Enloe's boy. Enloe gave Tom Lincoln a mare, mule, and $15 for his efforts, and the three went back to Lynn Mountain in Carter County, Tennessee, where they stayed until going to Kentucky.

A Judge Gilmore quoted by Judge Alley says he knew Nancy Hanks before she married Thomas Lincoln, and that she had a child she called Abraham. After Thomas Lincoln and Nancy Hanks were married, the lad was known as Abraham Lincoln, Gilmore swore in an affidavit. Judge Gilmore practiced law for sixty years and said he never heard the question of Abraham Lincoln's illegitimacy disputed. The man who reportedly married the couple said Nancy had a son large enough to run around when he performed the ceremony.

Judge Alley refers to attorney William Herndon's biography and to other family members in building the background of Nancy Hanks. Herndon quoted Dennis Hanks, first cousin of Nancy, in his book. The story is tangled. This is one of the reasons Lincoln biographers and historians reject the Enloe and Calhoun theories. However, Judge Alley noted that while he could not qualify as an expert on the subject of "the way of a man with a maid," he could—by virtue of his long experience as a lawyer and judge in the mountains—form an intelligent opinion and reach a definite conclusion about questions of family relationships after a fair and impartial investigation of the facts. President Lincoln himself said, according to Judge Alley's quote of the 1860 Hicks biography by Warren,

> I was born February 12, 1809, in the then Hardin County, Kentucky, at a point within the now County of LaRue, a mile or a mile and a half from where Hodgen's Mill now is. My parents being dead, and my own memory not serving, I know of no means of identifying the precise locality.

Judge Alley found various witnesses who placed the birthplace in Western North Carolina, not Kentucky. The President admitted he had no memory of ever hearing of the place or event. Alley reported that the witnesses to both the Calhoun and Tennessee tradition were men of position and character.

While Abraham Enloe's behavior, that of his wife, and Nancy Hanks tends to support the Enloe family tradition, Alley suggests other motives. Nancy Hanks had lived in the Enloe household and Abraham Enloe was her surrogate father, and he reacted in a fatherly way while at the same time had problems at home based on Nancy's pregnancy. Mrs. Enloe refused to speak to him, and it was tearing up the house. He was willing to do anything to restore peace to the Enloe household. Hence, he hired Tom Lincoln to take Nancy away. As to the Enloe tradition, Alley asserts that neither

Nancy nor Enloe admitted to an affair, while the Calhoun family members aware of the situation agree that John C. Calhoun and Nancy Hanks did admit to an affair in front of family members. The testimony was that of Calhoun family members, and thus within the family tradition.

Historians say the dates of who was where and when conflict in the stories. Judge Alley cast his lot with the Calhoun family tradition rather than the Enloe story. Historians cast their lot with Lincoln's memory of an entry in a family Bible, which according to him shed no light on the question. Whatever the truth of the matter, the tale persists in the Blue Ridge and Great Smokies and is told again and again whenever folks gather. Only if it is possible to gather evidence based on DNA will the mystery ever be solved. As in the case of the Jefferson family, the oral tradition, while based on hearsay evidence, does carry weight with descendants. In the folklore of the Great Smokies, the birth and parentage of President Abraham Lincoln is a twice-told tale.

The House on the Hill—Biltmore

When George Washington Vanderbilt vacationed for health reasons in Asheville in 1888, Western North Carolina was still pretty much isolated from the rest of the country. Its lofty mountains—the Blue Ridge on the east, Great Smokies to the west, and the Blacks just north along with the Unicoi—still had not been ravaged by timber men; its roads were still rough wagon trails; and its backwoods people considered by some to be peculiar. It was still a frontier of sorts that had potential for those with an eye to the future. And it had beauty—awesome beauty.

Western North Carolina also had a budding health industry centered around the little town of Asheville based on pure mountain air and water, good food, a relaxing atmosphere, and a good climate. The word most often used to describe the mountain climate was *salubrious*.

George Vanderbilt could afford to travel to remote places for his health. His grandfather, the famous Commodore Cornelius Vanderbilt, born in 1794 of Staten Island farmers and boat owners, had parlayed a small sailboat purchased for $100 borrowed from his mother when he was sixteen into a shipping and railroad empire worth more than $100 million before he died in 1877. He became one of the titans of American business headquartered in New York City before and after the Civil War. George's father, William Henry Vanderbilt, one of thirteen children, inherited the bulk of the Commodore's fortune. He, in turn, proceeded to increase the $100 million fortune to $200 million through expansion of the New York Central Railroad, four other railroads, and coal mining.

While Commodore Vanderbilt was a rough and ready shipping and railroad magnate, his son, William Henry, was an outstanding railroad man, polished financier, and art patron. In fact, William Henry, the Commodore's eldest son, inherited the family fortune only because his younger brother, Cornelius Jeremiah Vanderbilt, had long been in disfavor with his father. As some historians note, he was not good at making and holding money. The younger brother, Cornelius Jeremiah, also liked the good life while his brother, William Henry, was an "industrious plodder, who scrupulously avoided the haunts of gentlemen and had a reverence for money and a real talent for holding on to it."

The Commodore considered making and saving money a virtue and losing in the gaming houses and spending it on beautiful women a vice. The old Commodore may have been tough, irascible, and stubborn, but it was no accident that when he died the richest man in the United States on January 4, 1877, the family stood around the bed singing, "Come Ye Sinners, Poor and Needy."

George's father, William (Billy) Henry Vanderbilt, earned his place as the inheritor of the old Commodore's legacy the hard way: by working for it. Born in New Brunswick, New Jersey, in 1821 when his mother was operating a stagecoach inn and his father a steamship line, Billy Vanderbilt didn't enter the family business after education at Columbia College because his father didn't think much of his ability. Instead, he went to sea as a ship chandler's clerk. That didn't really interest him either, so he became a bank clerk at $1,000 a year and married a shy girl he met in Sunday school, Maria Louisa Kissam. Her family is what in those days they called *good stock.* A fine background. Miss Kissam's father was a minister of the Dutch Reformed Church and her ancestors were distinguished in colonial times as lawyers, merchants and ministers. Despite these facts, the Commodore objected to the marriage, so he did not give the young couple a wedding present. A penny saved on wedding presents is a penny earned, to paraphrase Benjamin Franklin.

Billy worked in a bank near Albany, New York, for three years before his health broke down. The family doctor suggested fresh air and a new occupation. Commodore Vanderbilt, disgusted, gave his son just enough money to purchase a broken-down seventy-acre farm in the town of New Dorp on Staten Island. The Commodore was amazed when William Henry turned a profit on the farm in a year and was able to purchase more land. The Commodore decided to test him further and made him receiver for the bankrupt Staten Island Railroad. The son not only put the railroad back on its feet, but he paid off all claims against it.

By now William Henry was forty-three years of age and blooming. He was given a new assignment by his father, the vice presidency of the New York & Harlem Railroad. Upon his father's death, William Henry became president of the New York Central Hudson River Railroads, which later he combined with the Lake Shore and Michigan Southern and Michigan Central to form the New York Central System. William Henry Vanderbilt, father of George, also put together a number of pieces of property in New York and then built the largest, grandest, most elegant house in the United States at the most elegant address in the country, Fifth Avenue, New York City. George Vanderbilt's father also was a patron of the arts including paintings, sculpture, and architecture. Thus, elegance became second nature for George Vanderbilt.

George was the youngest child of Maria Kissam and William Henry Vanderbilt, and he was completely different from his brothers and sisters. Instead of money, George Vanderbilt was a student of languages, art, landscaping, literature, and philosophy. He could speak eight different languages and was able to read several others including Indian dialects. Records note that he often accompanied his father abroad on art-buying trips. Instead of public or private schooling, he was tutored at home.

In every sense of the word, George Vanderbilt was a connoisseur and collector of fine art, tapestries, jewels, books, and furniture. He inherited the family's Fifth Avenue property and had residences at Bar Harbor, Maine, and New Dorp. George was close to his father, and shortly before William Henry's death, the two men went to New Dorp to check on the farm which supplied fruit, vegetables, and flowers for the family's Fifth Avenue mansion and to observe progress on the Vanderbilt Mausoleum which was being built at the Moravian Cemetery there. Five days later, William Henry Vanderbilt, who had earlier turned his business interests over to associates because of failing health, died of a stroke. He was buried at the Mausoleum at New Dorp, and George came into the money he was to use to build the greatest, grandest, and most elegant country house in all America.

Not only did George Vanderbilt inherit money from his father and mother, but he also inherited the love of art and beautiful things. So when he visited Asheville for his health and saw the vistas, George Vanderbilt fell in love with the mountains and the salubrious climate. He decided to build his country place at the little crossroads village of Best just south of Asheville. As his grandfather and father before him, George Vanderbilt knew a bargain when he saw one. So he had his agent, Charles McNamee—later to be manager of Biltmore, quietly buy up fifty worn-out farms and eight impoverished antebellum estates on 7,270 acres of land in and around the village of Best.

The decay and social decadence of the antebellum estates was a direct result of the Civil War's impact on the fortunes of those wealthy planters and cotton factors from Charleston and Savannah who summered in the mountains to escape the heat and malaria of the low country. They let the buildings go because of the lack of money and slaves after the war, which led also to a stagnation of the society in general. Owners of the farms thought the land agents slightly daft for wanting to purchase their worn-out farms and decaying houses. Long ago the land had been denuded of trees. Where crops once grew in abundance, gullies wrinkled the land overgrown with sedge grass. Each year the owners of the land had burned the land in a primitive farming practice that leaves the topsoil barren of mulch for future crops.

It was the custom of the day to wear out farms, leave, and carve out yet another farm in the Western Carolina wilderness until that farm, too, gave out. The pattern was slash, burn, grow, and leave. When someone came along and offered cash for worn-out land, the farmers and estate owners figured the money was a bonus in the established pattern of life. George Vanderbilt, on the other hand, had a vision. First, he would build a country house that reflected his concept of civilized taste and style. Second, he would reclaim the land from its present condition and make money at the same time, long a family trait. It still is. Members of the vast Vanderbilt clan consider houses, lawns, gardens, and elegant living their heritage even today. His home away from Fifth Avenue would be on a grand scale to match the mountains and his fortune.

Thus came into being what is now known as Biltmore, the most spectacular mansion in America; Biltmore Forest, a successful experiment in conservation; and Pisgah Forest, the Cradle of Forestry in America. Both the public lands and private Biltmore Estate are a legacy to the people of the United States because of the Vanderbilt's concept of heritage and stewardship of that heritage.

What was wrought by George Vanderbilt with his inheritance? For starters, Asheville, Western North Carolina, and the village of Best would never be the same again, neither would the forestry and timber industry. The village of Best had a railroad—a necessity where the Vanderbilts were concerned—to get back and forth to New York in their private railroad car, a general store, a post office, and some houses when George Vanderbilt decided to buy the surrounding land. He discovered it while horseback riding one afternoon during his stay at the Kenilworth Inn. In buying the surrounding land, George Vanderbilt also purchased himself a town on the banks of the Swannanoa River which flows into the French Broad River. He renamed the place Biltmore Village, and it has been that on the maps and railroad timetable ever since. George Vanderbilt also built new village buildings and stores, as well as a church, All Souls Episcopal, in the architecture of a Swiss village. He headquartered his house and farm operations in the village.

Of course, he needed a house to go with the acreage his agent had purchased, so he contacted the family architect in New York, Richard Morris Hunt, and told him he wanted a house on a hill overlooking both the Swannanoa and French Broad rivers, the forest lands, and a vista of the highest mountain near Asheville, Mount Pisgah, which he also had purchased in his quest for a place in the mountains.

Hunt was one of the most famous architects in America. Well born to a father who was a congressman and a mother who was known for her beauty and artistic talent, Hunt was taken early to France for his health. It was there Hunt, who had planned to go to

West Point, changed career paths and entered the Ecole des Beaux-Arts in Paris. He was the first American to go through the rigors of Beaux-Arts architectural training. His training and travel around France to chateaux, palaces, churches, and public monuments fired in him a desire to return to the United States and awaken his fellow citizens to the beauties of the arts. As art critic and author Russell Lynes has observed, this meant the arts of Europe.

He knew the rich and famous of the day, and, because he was easy to get along with, they hired him to design their houses. His impact was enormous because he believed, "the first thing you've got to remember is that it's your client's money you are spending. Your business is to get the best results you can, following their wishes. If they want you to build a house upside down, standing on its chimney, it's up to you to do it and to get the best possible results." Hunt's famous designs include The Breakers or Marble House in Newport, Rhode Island; the pedestal for the Statue of Liberty; Administration Building for the Chicago World's Fair of 1893; and, of course, Biltmore.

George Vanderbilt, a shy bachelor of twenty-six whose slight, slender build, dark complexion and pencil moustache made him look very French, knew he wanted a southern home to display many of his art treasures, but he had not settled on a concept yet. However, Vanderbilt also knew he liked the Loire Valley in France. When Hunt came and saw the French Broad and Swannanoa rivers coming together in the valley, he immediately thought of the Loire too. The site determined the commission.

The commission: design a chateau in the French Renaissance manner, much like Chateau de Blois in France. Oh yes, one other point: the chateau was to have all of the modern conveniences of that day. For Hunt, who designed many of the family's two dozen or so "castles" at outposts of elegance such as Bar Harbor, Long Island, Newport, Fifth Avenue, and the Adirondacks, the commission for Biltmore meant a masterpiece. It also meant America's largest commission for a house with 255 rooms and forty-five baths. But then, little did Hunt know that George Vanderbilt's grandson would be inviting seven hundred thousand paying guests a year to visit Biltmore and most of them would be flushing the toilets. He also wouldn't have known that ten thousand of them would want to come the day after Thanksgiving to view the house in its

Christmas splendor, and the wait would be more than two hours long before visitors could enter the front door and great hall.

When visitors enter the house today, they are as awed as in George Vanderbilt's day. The winter garden is a profusion of flowers and plants. Off to a side is a billiard room where George Vanderbilt and friends played billiards and other pastimes favored by gentlemen. A hidden panel in the billiard room opens, revealing the smoking room where male guests retired to sip brandy and smoke clear La Habana cigars after dinner or a game of billiards. The gun room, containing the weapons of the hunt, was also off the billiard room.

The banquet room is almost overwhelming. It has arches seventy feet in the air, is seventy feet by forty-two feet in length and width, and seats twenty-six for dinner easily, and thirty-eight to forty if extra leaves are placed in the long table. The room is acoustically perfect. That means you can sit at one end of the table and speak in a normal voice, and a person at the other end can hear as if you were sitting side by side. There is a huge fireplace at one end. The decorations are medieval trophies of armor with replicas of the thirteen original state or colonial flags of the colonies along with the Biltmore World War I flag. Did the family eat in the great hall every day? Of course not. The great hall was used when guests were in attendance. The family dining room, called the breakfast room, seats eight. It is also quite elegant.

There is a morning salon, where the ladies met to talk, a music room, another room which might be considered the main salon or living room, (called the tapestry room because of its tapestries), and the library. The latter, acclaimed as one of the most magnificent private libraries in the world, is where George Vanderbilt, owner and builder of Biltmore, spent most of his time when in residence. Remember, he was a scholar, and libraries are to scholars as concert halls are to musicians. George Vanderbilt could delve into the great books of the time, study, think, and contemplate the issues of the day in his library.

All of the rooms have magnificent furniture and works of art. Some of the furniture was made at a furniture factory George Vanderbilt set up in Biltmore Village when he arrived. In recent years the Biltmore Company has set up a restoration shop where both art works and the furniture are restored by craftsmen trained to old-world standards. Upstairs are the bed and sitting rooms, all of which seem more like apartments than bedrooms for sleeping. There is a north bedroom—the one used by George's mother at first and later by his wife, Edith Stuyvesant Dresser; a south bedroom, Vanderbilt's room; and various guest rooms. In addition, you had what they call the oak sitting room, Old English room, Chippendale room, Sheraton room, Halloween room, and a men's gym. There is an indoor pool (now empty), bowling alley, and game room in the basement. George Vanderbilt's personal bath is unique in that it was the finest the 1890s could offer, with indoor plumbing at a time when most people had a privy. The kings and queens of Europe, who used chamberpots, did not live so well.

Yes, there is also an upstairs-downstairs segregation to the house. In days past, the name was servants' quarters, little rooms off narrow hallways where there was a social pecking order far more rigid than in the upstairs part of the house. Kitchens for this and that, a buttery, commissary, linen rooms, bakery, wine cellar, laundry, shops, and offices of the various stewards and personnel, are all part of the downstairs area now open to the public. To some, the house comes into perspective more in the servants' quarters than upstairs where the beauty and elegance is somewhat overwhelming.

What visitors don't see are the huge furnaces, the electrical power plant George Vanderbilt had put in to produce electricity for light, and the pipes and wires going everywhere. It is the technical stuff of which small cities are made.

Architect Richard Morris Hunt decided that for a proper Renaissance chateau the building material should be limestone. So he ordered the limestone from Indiana, some six hundred miles away. It arrived by train in Asheville, and then the railroad cars were shunted over a spur track leading right to the house. The railroad spur was removed once the house was finished. Mr. Vanderbilt also built a brick factory with kilns, a band sawmill, sidings, and warehouses to go with the furniture factory along the tracks to Asheville, so his new estate would have these products for construction. It took one thousand artisans and workmen to build and landscape Biltmore, what some have called "an army of workmen."

There were a number of problems facing Hunt, none greater than George Vanderbilt's desire to locate his castle in the sky at a certain place so his back porch could look out toward Mount Pisgah. The problem was that the site where Vanderbilt wanted the house was a valley, not a promontory. Remember, one of the reasons people of wealth, the Vanderbilts included, hired Richard Morris Hunt in the first place was his problem-solving abilities. He did what the client wanted. So when George Vanderbilt chose the site in a valley instead of a promontory overlooking the French Broad River Valley toward Mount Pisgah, Hunt suggested they fill in the valley to make a promontory. And they did, hauling by drag pan, rail, and wagon enough rock and dirt to fill in the valley and set Biltmore high above the surrounding land. It was quite an undertaking just filling the valley to say nothing of building the Indiana limestone castle with its 255 rooms, turrets designed from three different French chateaus, and millions of brick and thousands of feet of wood paneling from the great forests in the distance.

George Vanderbilt's kith and kin never blinked nor considered George odd. They had done or were doing the same thing, building pleasure domes with the greatest of fancies. Commodore Vanderbilt would have snorted if he had seen what his progeny was doing. Even at the peak of his wealth and power, the old Commodore preferred "sodey water" to champagne because, he said, both had bubbles, and soda water was cheaper if it was bubbles you wanted.

The house, when completed, would be three times larger than the White House. With the house going up, George Vanderbilt had another problem: what to do about front, side, and back yards? Hire a landscaper. Mr. Vanderbilt did. He was Frederick Law Olmsted, the designer of Central Park in New York City. Central Park was considered Olmsted's triumph up until that time. Biltmore would be an encore, and what an encore it would be. In fact, the encore would be better than the earlier triumph, and larger. The yard of Biltmore would be nine times larger than Central Park.

Olmsted took one look at the worn-out farmlands upon which the estate stood and began work. Reforestation began immediately. The sedge grass along the French Broad River bottoms was removed. Olmsted's plan called for a large arboretum with more species of trees than in the famous Kew Gardens in London. Traversing the arboretum would be ten miles of macadamized roads, that era's blacktop. It turned out the roads wouldn't be blacktopped until much later. The rundown houses and cabins on the land were removed. There wasn't a marketable tree in the acres of woodlands surrounding the estate. The main job of workmen for a while was the removal of the chestnut trees and stumps hit hard by the infamous chestnut blight. These trees provided wood to fire the brick kilns used to make the brick used in building the house. It was planned to have large tree nurseries along the Swannanoa River to replenish the trees gone from the estate.

A dairy farm, pig farm, and poultry farm were also under construction. The dairy farm became the famous Biltmore Dairy Farms of later years. Today the dairy is closed, and in its place is the Biltmore Winery. Some of the farm buildings may be seen today on the long drive out of the estate.

The house and gardens are perhaps the most beautifully landscaped in America today. Biltmore's greenhouses provide flowers for the house. The gardens are designed to have flowers all summer. In fact, many people visiting Biltmore spend more time in the gardens than they do in the house.

With Olmsted in charge of the arboretum, it became natural that some thought would be given to the forest lands. George Vanderbilt hired the famous forester, Gifford Pinchot, to be a consultant on the forest he wanted on the acreage. Eventually the 7,220 acres would grow to 125,000 acres and take in parts of counties to the west and south. Pisgah Forest is the name given this forest, some ten miles from Biltmore and extending sixty miles to the west. Pinchot was the man for the job. He had put together New York's Adirondack Park in the northern part of the state. He also was America's first trained forester and later governor of Pennsylvania. Although Pinchot stayed at the Kenilworth Inn while working at Biltmore, much of his time was spent in the field trying to come up with a comprehensive forest plan for George Vanderbilt that would combine nursery, reforestation, and harvest in an ongoing project.

Pinchot's plan was to harvest and market timber, using splash dams on creeks to contain logs until they could be floated down the French Broad River to a band mill. Unfortunately, the splash dams didn't work. The market for timber and lumber was depressed, and when the price did go up, the trees were difficult to get out. In addition, Pinchot had opened an office as a consulting forester in New York with Vanderbilt's permission, and that took some of his time away from consultations at Biltmore.

Pinchot, a religious person who often preached Sundays in local churches, was depressed over the death of his fiancée. He privately told friends he wanted to leave. In 1894, Pinchot suggested a German forester named Carl A. Schenck to Vanderbilt as one who might undertake to bring some order out of the chaos that existed in what would become Biltmore Forest. In addition to his depression, Pinchot had other projects and could not stay at Biltmore to oversee the progress. Dr. Schenck came highly recommended, so George Vanderbilt agreed to a contract of $2,500 a year, two saddle horses, feed for the horses, and a house. Schenck wanted his pay in gold, but Vanderbilt said that would be impossible if William Jennings Bryan should be elected President of the United States in the fall of 1896. Bryan was a Democrat who campaigned against the use of the gold standard with a speech called "The Cross of Gold."

Vanderbilt also refused one other request made by Schenck: he would not pay for a topographical map for the 100,000 acres he owned outside of Biltmore Forest because he had paid $30,000 for the Biltmore Forest map, and he thought the price too high and that he had been taken. A sketch map had been made, and he thought that enough. Schenck told Vanderbilt forestry was a matter of transportation, and to build good roads you have to have a good topo map. No map. George Vanderbilt may have looked French; but he was Dutch on both sides of his family, and he could be stubborn when given the opportunity.

There is the story told many years later that when George Vanderbilt's grandsons were in charge of the estate, the Federal government began negotiations for the route across Biltmore Forest for the Blue Ridge Parkway. Negotiations were difficult, and each time a new local Parkway official or one from Washington would take part, the person wanted to see the house. The brothers became aware that, in addition to negotiating, they were running a free tourist attraction for the visiting government brass. They decided to move negotiations along the next time the government men came, so they made them pay the entrance fee at the gate in order to come in and talk. That happened only a few more times before the government settled, and the Parkway was built across Biltmore Estate. Commodore Vanderbilt smiled down on his progeny, it is said around Biltmore Village.

Charles McNamee, Biltmore's general manager and George Vanderbilt's agent in securing the lands, came up with an idea to work around the cost of the maps. He was a good friend of the head of the U.S. Geological Survey, and he knew that the Pisgah Quadrangle, among the maps of the geological survey, was about to be redrawn. For a contribution the maps were drawn, and Schenck agreed to become the forester for Biltmore. Schenck's men built two hundred miles of trails for the surveyors, and the maps produced were excellent. He also cleared some roads to bring out the timber, but the splash dam idea continued and was a disaster. There were some other problems. George Vanderbilt wanted hardwoods planted immediately on fields around the estate. So Schenck and his men planted thousands of acorns and seed nuts. Alas, they failed to come up the next spring. He had not figured on the field mice and squirrels. They ate the seed. There were no nurseries in the area, so Schenck ordered seedlings from Germany. They were planted and grew.

Out of that experience, in a roundabout way, came the idea for a School of Forestry. George Vanderbilt wanted a hunting lodge built in the Buckspring area of this newly acquired forest. Schenck really didn't want to build because he needed housing for his workers, but Vanderbilt didn't want the workers living on the estate. So they lived in different small communities around the estate, some as far away as Asheville itself. This resulted in hardship for the workers and apprentices, so, whenever they thought they knew enough to obtain other forest employment, they left. To curry favor for an idea he had, Schenck went all out to build and complete Buckspring Lodge, and for many years it was the hunting lodge for the family. Today the site is on the Blue Ridge Parkway about a mile north of Pisgah Inn and the campground. There is a parking lot and trail to the site of the lodge.

This problem of worker turnover led Schenck to propose the idea he had been preparing Vanderbilt to accept — a school for the apprentices in the Pink Beds. Vanderbilt went along with the idea as a result of Schenck's efforts at Buckspring, and the first School of Forestry in the United States was established with Dr. Schenck as its director and chief instructor. Today, visitors to Pisgah National Forest may visit the museum and its buildings from both Brevard and the Blue Ridge Parkway.

It would be nice to say the forestry work was a success, but it wasn't. Lumber prices, depression, and a number of other problems kept the program from operating in the black. Try as he might, Schenck was unable to make the forest profitable. Oh yes, there were good years when a few dollars were made on this or that, but the long run looked bleak. Schenck and Pinchot continued their efforts with Schenck interested in a major Appalachian Park for much of the lands. It was during this period that George Vanderbilt took a decided interest in Pisgah Forest. Many times he invited guests to camp with him and his party in the forest. Schenck decided to build better camping facilities for Vanderbilt. More roads were built, and the forest had potential of becoming a paying endeavor. Schenck was even upbeat at times.

The depression of 1902 was the turning point. George Vanderbilt lost heavily on the stock market. Bills began to mount, and there was no money to pay them. Vanderbilt sold his horses and closed the stables. He sold his private railroad car. All work on the estate stopped. McNamee, the general manager, resigned—no work. The Vanderbilts sailed for Europe, spending 1903 there. It was less expensive there than in the United States. New York Central stock, basis of the Vanderbilt fortune, declined 30 percent in a few weeks. Biltmore, which cost $6,000 a month in 1902 to run, was closed.

There were attempts to lease Pisgah Forest to the Kenilworth Inn as a hunting and fishing preserve for wealthy businessmen, but the efforts failed. Schenck decided to visit his home in Germany. When he returned, the school had continued to do well, but the "lumber trade was in the claws of the devil." One day Vanderbilt told Schenck that he (Vanderbilt) was done with forestry and that someone else might take up where he left off. "Try to sell Pisgah Forest for me," he told Schenck. "I will pay you the usual agent's commission on the purchase price."

Schenck perceived that the house would be a white elephant without the forest, so he did little. In his memoirs, Schenck was sad that his experiment with a self-sufficient forest based on the growing and harvesting of timber did not succeed. In 1909, with still no improvement in timber sales, Schenck could see the end coming. He concentrated on his forestry school while problems mounted. When he received a legacy from Germany, he resigned. Two forests, Biltmore and Pisgah, had been established; a forestry school, the first in America, had been established at Biltmore; George Vanderbilt had been the patron of the school and forests. Today they stand as a monument to his vision.

Despite the financial problems of her husband, Mrs. Vanderbilt established a school at Biltmore which taught domestic arts and crafts to mountain women and their daughters. Emphasis was placed on wool products. In 1917, the school was purchased by the Grove Park Inn, and today the shops are a museum and store where fine woolens can be purchased. Mrs. Vanderbilt also established the annual Christmas Party for employees of Biltmore and their children. It is a much anticipated annual event even today.

The Vanderbilts maintained a home, among others, in Washington. There, in March of 1914, Mr. Vanderbilt underwent an appendectomy and later died of a pulmonary embolism following the operation. The trust fund left to him by his father went to his daughter, Cornelia, then fourteen years of age. Biltmore, the estate, land, and cash went to his wife, Edith. Mrs. Vanderbilt made a decision to keep Pisgah Forest intact, and it was sold to the United States Forestry Commission to become the nucleus of what is known today as Pisgah National Forest. A total of five hundred acres around Buckspring Lodge and twelve thousand acres surrounding Biltmore, the Biltmore Forest, was exempt from the sale to the government.

Upon the death of her mother, Cornelia (Tarheel Nell) Stuyvesant Vanderbilt inherited Biltmore and the estate. She had married the Hon. John Francis Cecil, son of Col. Lord William Cecil, C.V.O., gentleman Usher to the King, late Comptroller to Princess Henry of Battenberg, and a grandson of the third Marquess of Exeter. The C.V.O. is a distinguishing honor still given today in Britain, instituted by Queen Victoria as the Commander of the Royal Victorian Order, and awarded at various levels for outstanding personal services rendered to the monarchy. The Cecils had two sons, George H. V. Cecil and William A. V. Cecil. John Cecil, who, except for the seven years he was Minister of Information for England, operated Biltmore until his death in 1954. The house was opened to visitors during his stewardship. Upon their mother's death, George received the Biltmore Farms and part of the estate, and William received the house and part of the estate known as Biltmore Forest.

Today Biltmore is a major business. It is headquartered in downtown Asheville in a building designed by I. M. Pei, the famous architect, which William Cecil purchased for considerably less than its building price when Akzona Corporation ran into financial trouble. Biltmore House is managed as a corporation, not as a family house open to visitors. His daughter and son are executives with the Biltmore Company. It is operated without any tax breaks, federal grants, or subsidies. Biltmore pays its way and is a huge contributor both directly and indirectly to the Asheville and Western North Carolina economy.

Biltmore is considered a national treasure, and it is. The finest private home ever built in America: George Vanderbilt's country house on a hill.

The White Chief Who Saved the Eastern Band of Cherokees

The story of the Cherokee Nation is a tragic one yet, especially when it is told that there are a dozen or so men, women, and chiefs who stand out as noble human beings. One of them is Col. William H. Thomas, the white chief who saved the Eastern Band, not once but thrice. His story is one of loyalty to the people who adopted him and his battle to preserve a people's heritage, culture, and lives through the most trying times anyone can face—ethnic cleansing 1830s style.

William Holland Thomas was born February 5, 1805, at Raccoon Creek, just north of Waynesville, North Carolina. He died May 10, 1893, at his daughter's home in Morganton, North Carolina, revered and honored among the older Cherokees as the man who created the Qualla Reservation of the Eastern Band of Cherokees by buying the land in his name when the Cherokees could not own land. He negotiated the surrender of Tsali, known as "Charley" by the townspeople and the military, and his brothers after they had killed three soldiers, thus paving the way for those hiding in the mountains to remain in a compromise he worked out with Gen. Winfield Scott. Tsali's surrender is the basis of the outdoor drama, Unto These Hills, performed each summer at the outdoor theater in Cherokee, North Carolina. The third event in which Will Thomas participated in an effort to save his Cherokee brothers came during the Civil War when he organized and commanded the famed "Thomas Legion" of Confederate troops. This enabled him to keep the Cherokee soldiers on duty in eastern Tennessee and Western North Carolina rather than fighting in the major battles in Virginia, thus saving the lives of the Cherokee volunteers on the Confederate side. As Indian agent, he also named the various towns encompassing the Qualla Reservation and set up a model government for the Cherokees to follow. However, it was his purchase of land for the Cherokees in his name when they could not own land that made him an icon in Cherokee history.

Will Thomas, first and only son of Richard and Temperance Calvert Thomas, was born into a harsh world. His father, relative of President Zachary Taylor, drowned trying to cross the Pigeon River near their home two months before Will was born. From his earliest days as a child he had to take responsibility. Small and quite intelligent, his mother educated him as she eked out a living in the valley. Helping his mother raise him were her husband's cousins, John and George Strother; an in-law, David Nelson; and the Colvard family.

At twelve or thirteen years of age he was engaged by Atty. Felix Walker of Waynesville to operate a trading store on Soco Creek near the present town of Cherokee. It was an early age to leave home to manage a store where furs, hides, and ginseng were brought in by the Indians for the China trade and exchanged for salt and other staples. His agreement to operate the store specified room and board and $100 at the end of three years. At the end of the three years Walker didn't have the money to pay Thomas the $100 for his services. Walker did have some old law books in his office in Waynesville, so he offered them to Thomas in lieu of money for his services. Thomas pondered the unusual payment but went ahead with the deal. It proved to be the basis for his fame and fortune. Thomas began the study of law by reading the books, and they provided the knowledge that he used to build a fortune and participate in Indian affairs. The reading of law, incidentally, was the way many a famous North Carolina attorney and judge originally became lawyers when law schools were scarce in the state, and far away from the mountains, as well as being elite and expensive. This reading of precedents and statutes allowed them to pass the state bar and to practice law. Incidentally, it was by this same method that Abraham Lincoln began to practice law as a young man. This practice of "reading the law" ended in the 1960s when the state moved to require a law degree of anyone sitting to take the bar exam.

There also were two other key elements in his operating the trading post at Quallatown: There was a Cherokee lad at the store who taught him to speak fluent Cherokee in his dealings with the tribe. One of the chiefs who traded at the store, Yonaguska, better known as Drowning Bear, was impressed with young Will Thomas' fairness and courtesy in dealing with his customers. So impressed was Yonaguska that when he found out Will had neither father nor brother, he asked the lad if he could adopt him. Will Thomas agreed and became a member of the Cherokee Nation, son of one of its powerful chiefs, Yonaguska. His tribal name was Wil-Usdi, or Little Will. He could speak the language, and, after the Cherokee syllabary came into use, he learned to write the language as well.

All of this and the fact that Will Thomas was an outstanding trader set the stage for the future. In 1820, when he was unemployed, his adoptive father, Chief Yonaguska, asked the youngster to aid him in tribal legal matters. He did, gaining confidence day by day in the field of law. In 1822, when he was seventeen years of age, Little Will acquired the Quallatown store from James and Polly Sherill Conley. A settlement had grown up around the store. Because Cherokees could not pronounce the P in Polly, or Pollytown, the name became Qually, or Quallytown. It was located at the confluence of Soco Creek and the Oconaluftee River in the present area of Cherokee. Will Thomas was on his way. He acquired seven more trading posts over the years, a wagon factory in Waynesville, and a tannery near Dillsboro. He acquired 150,000 acres of land with his own and tribal money which became the basis of the present-day Cherokee Reservation.

When the Cherokees sold their lands along the Tuckasegee in 1819, Will Thomas moved his home to property near the confluence of Soco Creek and the Oconaluftee a short distance from the property of Chief Yonaguska and the trading post. Thomas also brought his mother from Waynesville to live with him. The Cherokees who lived along the Tuckasegee River retreated west of the Nantahalas to what is now Graham County and Robbinsville when their lands were sold. Others stayed along the Oconaluftee. The Soco store prospered. The store owner being an adopted son of the chief didn't hurt either.

The Cherokee Nation's system of tribal leadership includes three chiefs, serving simultaneously, but being involved in different areas of the tribe's affairs, namely peace, war, and medicine. Chief Yonaguska was a counseling "peace chief," rather than a war chief of the Cherokees, in the most isolated section of the Cherokee Nation. As a result, his name does not appear in the records of the negotiations or meetings involving those who favored removal and those who did not, since as peace chief, his job was to give wisdom and counsel to the war chiefs, who would then do the actual negotiating. Chief Yonaguska was the best orator of all the chiefs, and when he did attend the councils and meetings of the national government at New Echota in Georgia he pleaded the case against removal.

When the Tuckasegee lands were sold, Yonaguska purchased a 650-acre reservation between Cherokee and Bryson City as his home. He intended the land to be Cherokee until his dying day. Today a portion of that land has been purchased by the Cherokee Nation. The chief also ended the sale and use of liquor by the Eastern Band after finding it addictive and damaging to his people. He made an eloquent speech before the council in which he pointed out the evils of liquor. His audience was moved to tears. He had Little Will write out a pledge, and each chief signed, as well as each individual in the entire nation, thus ending the use of whiskey by the Eastern Band. He also hewed to traditional ways, and when the Christian missionaries came from New England and Pennsylvania to convert the Cherokee to Christianity, he forbade the reading of the Bible printed in the Cherokee syllabary at New Echota until it had been read to him and found to be a good book. He did make one telling comment: "Well, it seems to be a good book—strange that the white people are not better, after having it so long."

As an adopted son of the most powerful counselor chief, Will Thomas was in his twenties when he was made Indian agent before the Removal. Before he died in 1838, Chief Yonaguska called the tribal council of the Eastern Band together to convince the elders to name his adopted son, Will Thomas, as chief in his place. The vote favored Thomas, and he became the white chief of the Eastern Band, enabling him to negotiate with both federal and state governments over the fate of the Eastern Band.

Will Thomas played two key roles in the Removal, both of which literally saved the Eastern Band and created the present-day reservation. The first came toward the end of the roundup of sixteen thousand Cherokees for removal to the Oklahoma Indian Territory. The other happened in the aftermath of the roundup.

Several motives for the Removal have been attributed to President Jackson throughout history, including the idea that he was unhappy with the Cherokee for their aiding of the British during the Revolutionary War. Certainly the Removal of the Cherokee was a complicated issue. Jackson himself used the excuse that a nation, in this case the conquered Cherokee Nation, could not exist within another nation, so the Cherokee nation and its people had to be removed. Gold was the real reason. It had been discovered by the Cherokees living in Dahlonega, Georgia, and the Georgians wanted it for themselves. In order to get it, they had the state pass a law confiscating all Cherokee lands in Georgia. The Georgians walked up to homes and farms owned by Cherokee Indians and actually threw out the people at gunpoint, taking over all Indian property and leaving the homeless owners to shift for themselves. The Georgians enlisted Jackson in their scheme, and he instigated the Removal to enhance his political survival in Washington by proposing the removal bill in 1829. It was a sordid story of man's inhumanity to man. The treaty of New Echota sealed the Cherokee Nation's fate, although fewer than five hundred out of sixteen thousand tribe members signed the treaty, intended to give the United States the power to remove the Cherokees from their lands. The actual removal began in 1838.

President Jackson officially ordered the army to round up the Cherokees in order to relocate them permanently to the Indian Territory of Oklahoma. The atrocities committed by some federal troops against the Indians, even from the beginning of the round-up, is well documented in many accounts. In the towns around the Great Smokies and other Western North Carolina mountains, resistance was great. Only residents of the lower and middle towns, people who had assimilated into white culture, agreed to abide with the removal order. Some Cherokees already rounded up broke out of the pens and stockades set up to hold them while the rest were hunted and captured for the forced march. About one thousand fled into the mountain fastness of the Great Smoky Mountains.

When it was obvious that the roundup, which took about three years, was going slowly because people were not volunteering to leave, the U.S. Army moved into Georgia, Tennessee, and Western North Carolina. Some seven thousand strong under Gen.Winfield Scott, they came with fixed bayonets on order from Scott to brook no nonsense during the relocation. Known by the Cherokee as the famous Trail of Tears, the forced march finally took place in the dead of winter to the Oklahoma Indian Territory in 1841. Most of the Indians made the twelve-hundred-mile cross-country trek on foot; many did not survive.

It was a brutal display of raw power instituted by President Andrew Jackson, an Indian hater, even though his life and career had been saved by six hundred Cherokee warriors at the Battle of New Orleans in 1814, the final battle of the War of 1812. In fact, the great Cherokee Chief Junaluska, the warrior who actually saved Jackson's life, told friends later that if he had known what President Jackson would do to the Cherokee in later years, he would have killed him at Horse Shoe Bend when he had the opportunity.

Will Thomas's first major act in the Removal came as the capturing of the Cherokees was coming to an end. During the roundup on the eastern slope of the Smokies, a group of soldiers pushed a little too hard with an Indian family headed by Charley (Tsali). Three soldiers were killed. Tsali, family, and followers headed back into the mountains in the Deep Creek area of the Smokies near Bryson City where they holed up in caves to escape the wrath of the army. Tsali and others who fled put themselves under the command of U'tsala, or Lichen, a noted leader, although Tsali remained with his people in his own personal hiding place. U'tsala and his people were starving in the caves. The leader lost his wife and children during this time, yet he and his followers preferred starvation in the familiar mountain fastness to bondage and the trek to Oklahoma.

The roundup was ending, and General Scott wanted out. He called upon Will Thomas to help him. If Thomas could get Tsali to surrender, Scott would call off the search and work out a compromise whereby the one thousand or so Cherokee in the mountains could remain. Little Will took with him several Indians and made his way by trail to the hiding place of U'tsala where he presented General Scott's idea. U'tsala considered the choices, either stay in the mountains and starve to death while General Scott turned all seven thousand soldiers loose in an effort to find the band, or surrender Tsali for punishment and save the remaining Indians. Thomas pointed out to the leader that by bringing Tsali to punishment under the rules of war, he could secure respite from the army's search-and-destroy mission for his followers. U'tsala pondered the proposition and the alternatives. He decided that if it took the sacrifice of three Cherokees to save one thousand, it was worth it. He told Thomas that while he was bitter, the proposition was the best way to save his people.

Rather than have U'tsala send the word to Tsali, Thomas undertook the mission himself. He trekked into the high country around Deep Creek until he found Tsali's hiding place. When he arrived he made sure to place himself between the guns of Tsali and his followers in front of the campfire. This conference was a remarkable event. Thomas spoke. Finally Tsali answered: "I will come in. I don't want to be hunted down by my own people."

Tsali, an old man by this time, bowed to the logic of saving his own people by self-sacrifice. In keeping with tribal culture and dignity, and because the army did not want to carry out the execution of the old man themselves, it was decided that the matter would be handled privately within the tribe. When Tsali and his people walked to his execution, it was to U'tsala and his followers in the mountains he went, not to the U.S. Army.

Will Thomas had done a remarkable job in presenting the alternatives. He also had saved the Eastern Band from extinction. The original New Echota treaty gave the Cherokee Nation $5 million, additional compensation for improvements to the land, additional money for the brutality of Georgians in claiming the land, and a per capita allowance to those making the trek to Oklahoma. President Jackson didn't agree and canceled the provisions that would enable some Cherokee to remain in their homeland. In short, President Jackson made Cherokees landless aliens within their home country.

In his second act as savior of the Cherokee Nation, Will Thomas then took up that fight in Washington, and for six years presented the Cherokee case before Congress and a new administration. He finally won. It was agreed that funds set aside for improvements and reservations would be transferred to Thomas as the Indian agent. He, in turn, set about purchasing tracts of land in Western North Carolina's mountains in his own name so the Cherokees could have a home. The land was placed in Thomas' name because neither North Carolina nor the federal government recognized Indian ownership of land. Years later when Will Thomas became mentally unstable due to old age, the courts, state, and federal government worked to unravel the complex land deals. In bringing order out of chaos, the Cherokee gained their present Qualla Reservation and other lands in the Snowbird Mountains.

Twice Little Will, adopted son of a chief, managed to snatch victory from the jaws of defeat. A third such event came during the Civil War, or what Will Thomas and others in the South called the War Between the States. Will Thomas believed in the Confederate cause of states' rights.

In what Horace Kephart later would call the "back of beyond," secession did not move many people whose main focus was to have shelter, eat three times a day, and eke out an existence via hunting, fishing, and a corn patch. As noted, it was a harsh world. Since few had slaves, slavery was not an issue. Until South Carolina seceded from the Union, North Carolina was counted as a Union state. Its mountain people, except for those in the towns, were Lincoln Republicans just as those in eastern Tennessee.

Thomas was at home with his tribe when a Confederate officer with Cherokee background visited the Great Smokies and painted a grand picture of war for the younger braves. The officer had a reputation for being reckless in an effort to make a name for himself. Thomas, although an old man, reacted by petitioning President Jefferson Davis, whom he knew from his days in Washington when Davis was a congressman, for permission to raise a regiment and command it. The outgrowth was "Thomas' Legion," consisting of one infantry regiment of ten companies, one infantry battalion of six companies, one cavalry battalion of eight companies, one field battery of artillery, and one company of engineers. All told, Colonel Thomas commanded twenty-eight hundred officers and men. This grew to more than four thousand as the war continued. The Legion, in accordance with Colonel Thomas' wishes, was used mostly as scouts and home guards on the eastern Tennessee and Western North Carolina border. The Legion was praised for its work for the Confederacy in the mountain passes and highlands.

Its only actual battle was at Baptist Gap in Tennessee where one of the Cherokee's best leaders was killed. The latent warrior instinct came out in these Indians who were now fighting for the Confederacy, and several Union soldiers were scalped by the Cherokees in their anger at losing their warrior leader. The Confederate command apologized for the scalpings. At war's end, the Legion's remaining units surrendered to the Union at Waynesville, and were allowed to keep their weapons and equipment. Colonel Thomas officially disbanded the Legion, and all went home. One footnote to history is that some Cherokee soldiers in the Legion were captured by Union forces and given the choice of prison camp or becoming Union soldiers. Most chose the latter. Professing disaffection for the Confederate government's treatment of Indians in the army, these war prisoners willingly joined the boys in blue after they had worn the gray. When they returned to the Smokies, they were given a very hard time by their former comrades in the Legion. Many soldiers made the same choice. Union prisons were as harsh as Confederate prisons.

The white chief had saved the tribe again by making sure its finest young men did not die in battle. It should be noted that many of the Legion's soldiers went home to become leaders and chiefs of the Eastern Band based on their work as noncommissioned officers. Col. Will Thomas came home, too. He was financially bankrupt. His trading posts had closed. He had spent great sums of money to feed the Qualla Cherokees who were starving. He was suffering from mental aberrations, and from time to time was confined to a Raleigh mental institution. At this point the courts, state, and federal government moved to untangle his financial affairs and make it possible for the Eastern Band to own their land.

Will Thomas also was one of the fathers of the Western North Carolina Railroad that was built from Asheville to Murphy. Those known as fathers of the railroad were men who offered ideas and advice for the development of the railroad, and who promoted it in the general assembly. The assembly then came up with the money to make the railroad a reality, based on that advice. The railroad was designed to provide a route to the midwest and to carry copper ore out of the Smokies to the smelter at Copperhill, Tennessee.

Col. William H. Thomas, now somewhat forgotten, was a remarkable mountain man—state senator, father of a railroad, Indian chief, Indian agent, and Confederate colonel. To the Cherokees, he was the white chief who saved a nation not once, but three times in one lifetime.

Carl Sandburg's Western North Carolina Home

One of the famous historic estates in Flat Rock, just south of Hendersonville, is Connemara, the last home of Lincoln biographer, author, journalist and poet Carl Sandburg. A far piece from Chicago, "hog butcher to the world," or the "sand-dune country" of Lake Michigan, both places Sandburg called home, Connemara and Flat Rock was the lair of the landed gentry. How an old hobo, who thought of himself poor even when he was financially wealthy, wound up in "Little Charleston in the Mountains" during the sunset of a distinguished career is well documented by Penelope Niven in her definitive biography of Carl Sandburg published in 1991. How the mountain people and townsfolk interacted with the famous international celebrity in their midst is a tale still largely untold.

The reason, of course, is mountain people, especially in Flat Rock and Hendersonville, have seen famous people come and go throughout the years on a regular basis. DuBose Heyward and George Gershwin wrote the play *Porgy and Bess* in Hendersonville;

world boxing champion Jack Dempsey trained in Laurel Park; F. Scott Fitzgerald wrote stories when he lived at the Skyland Hotel; and Gen. George C. Marshall visited regularly to confer with his mentor, Gen. Edward King, one of the Kings of Flat Rock. The list of famous people would take many pages if all were listed. Sandburg was one of many but unique in living the last twenty-two years of his life in the last bastion of the Confederacy, Connemara. For Lincoln's biographer, it was ironic.

Originally called Rock Hill, the estate was built between 1836 and 1838 by Christopher Memminger, first secretary of the treasury for the Confederacy in the cabinet of Jefferson Davis. Memminger was a lawyer from Charleston, South Carolina, who developed the phosphate fertilizer business in Charleston and a railroad into the Western North Carolina wilderness after being pardoned for his role in the Confederacy. He built the house so his family would have a cool summer residence where they could escape the stifling summers of the low country. Located five miles south of Hendersonville, Flat Rock became the retreat for many Charleston families such as the Memmingers. They built their estates on land once used by the Cherokee as a council grounds located atop and around a series of rock outcroppings—hence, the name Flat Rock. Their church, St. John-in-the-Wilderness, still stands today as one of the oldest churches in the area, and a relic of the old Confederacy amid the homes of wealthy newcomers who have turned the Hendersonville suburb into a series of upscale developments.

When Memminger failed to stabilize the Confederate economy, he resigned his wartime post and returned to Rock Hill, his 245-acre estate in the mountains. Memminger thought the mountains would be far to the rear of the fighting, since Charleston was where the Union was attempting to halt the blockade runners of the Confederacy. How wrong was his guess. Western North Carolina was divided, actually split asunder with neighbor against neighbor, family against family, and brother against brother in what Civil War historians are now discovering was the most inhumane guerrilla warfare in American history.

Hendersonville was predominately Union and Flat Rock Confederate. Connemara was not far from Farmer's Hotel (still operating and now called Woodfield Inn) where a company of Confederate home guards of the Sixty-fourth North Carolina under the command of Capt. B. T. Morris of Hendersonville tried to cope with difficulties caused by organized bands of deserters, as well as escaped Union prisoners of war from the Confederate prison camp in Spartanburg, called outliers, who raided local homes for money, goods, and food as they made their way to Knoxville, the closet Union-held location. There are still traces of the gun placements of these outliers in certain areas.

As the Confederacy began to collapse, President Jefferson Davis sent the Great Provisional Seal of the Confederacy to Memminger for safekeeping. In Richmond, the Davis government began to think of a place to which it could retreat. One place mentioned was Flat Rock, but the mountains, though normally a secure natural fortress, were not safe because its people were divided. Hendersonville had been taken over by outliers, and Captain Morris could not guarantee the safety of anyone, even on the mountainsides surrounding Flat Rock. In fact, as Davis and his cabinet fled south, Union cavalry under the command of Gen. George Stoneman were on a raid into North Carolina to disrupt communications, release Union prisoners held in Salisbury, and capture Jefferson Davis. One battalion of the Twelfth Ohio Volunteer Cavalry encamped at Hendersonville's old Judson College before receiving orders to head into South Carolina in an effort to capture the fleeing Davis.

Upon Memminger's death in 1888, members of the family sold Rock Hill to Capt. William Adger Smyth, a South Carolina textile manufacturer who moved to the mountains and opened Balfour Mills just north of Hendersonville during industrialization of the South after the Civil War. Captain Smyth renamed the estate Connemara after Connemara, Ireland, home of his ancestors. The green meadows, mists, and rock reminded him of Ireland. He died in 1942, and in 1945 the family placed the 243-acre estate on the market.

In the meantime, the Sandburgs had decided to move from the harsh winters in Michigan, and Mrs. Sandburg came to Asheville in quest of a farm where she could continue to raise goats and Mr. Sandburg could continue to write in retirement. One of the first places a real estate agent in Asheville mentioned was Connemara. The price, $45,000, was low to the Sandburgs while in the depressed market in Western North Carolina it was high. They purchased the farm and moved. The family had found the ideal place. The main house was apart from the barns; and there were meadows of lush grass, trails for hiking, stands of timber, and rock outcroppings for "seeing forever." For Carl Sandburg, the hurly-burly of Chicago was past; he had the solitude in which to work on novels, poetry, movie scripts, and memoirs. Mrs. Sandburg, daughters Margaret, Janet, and Helga, along with Helga's two children, Paula and John Carl, had their farm.

To Henderson County residents, the Sandburgs were just another famous family among many famous families who found the climate to their liking and stayed year 'round or just for the summer. Mrs. Sandburg made her trips to Francis & Wright, Hatch's, and the Farmer's Federation feed stores with Helga driving. The clerks liked her. Her goats became world champions, and the family operated a dairy that sold goat's milk in Hendersonville and Asheville. It is interesting to note that while Mrs. Sandburg's goats were capturing world titles, just a mile or so away at Crail Farm (now Crooked Creek Golf Club development), there were world-champion bulls being bred for the beef-cattle industry; and in Mills River the farms had the world's champion milk producers. Mills River is also the home of world-champion seed corn. The local newspaper, the *Times-News*, carried almost daily stories about the various champions, including the Sandburg goats. The paper also carried the news that Mrs. Sandburg attended meetings of the Home Demonstration Club and took part in farm-home programs.

Of course, goat breeding at the farm did set a few tongues to wagging in Hendersonville and Flat Rock. Rumors said the Sandburgs kept goats in the house. Actually, there was a birthing room in the basement of the house that was used in winter for newborn kids in order to enhance their survival. Baby goats, or kids, are among the most loveable creatures on earth, and when the birthing room was being used, the kids would often frolic around the Swedish stove that kept the basement warm in winter.

Sandburg made the obligatory treks to nearby Flat Rock High and Tuxedo Elementary schools for talks. Students thought him a funny old man because of his poetry. Most had never seen or heard a world-class writer, poet, or philosopher. In addition, Sandburg was a movie script writer and showman. Mountain children had never seen anything like him on stage as he sang and told stories.

Robert Morgan, now professor of English at Cornell University and a poet-novelist in his own right, remembers Mr. Sandburg coming to speak to his class. Morgan now makes those same treks as a scholar to interest young students in poetry and writing.

During his years at Connemara, Sandburg continued to write and produce a wealth of material. His novel, Remembrance Rock, was polished and honed at Connemara. Mail for Sandburg poured into the Flat Rock post office by the basketful in the late 1940s. Edward R. Murrow and CBS began the first of many interviews with the poet and writer. Other television networks would follow. He talked about the scripts he was doing for the movies. His writing hours were odd to the locals as he liked to work at night and meditate during the afternoons. Sometimes he would sit on a rock outcropping behind the antebellum house to think and write.

Most of Sandburg's writing was done in a plain room on the second floor of the house. He arranged his desk, orange-crate typewriter stand for his famous Remington typewriter, chair, bookshelves, and pencil holders so he could work much as he did when he lived in Michigan. Everything needed to write—paper, pencils, notes, etcetera—were within easy reach. Other writers and authors who visited him marveled at the setup. Downstairs was another office consisting of a table desk in one of the house's front rooms where he answered mail amid bookshelves housing part of his extensive library. He organized the mail answering with standardized answers. He put numbers on the mail so his secretaries would know which reply to use. Books, papers, and other items so precious to a writer spilled over all through the house and into the Swedish House. The Swedish House, still sitting on the property, is a two-story building near the main house that had the lines of houses and buildings in Sweden. Sandburg liked the lines, named it the Swedish House, and used it as a place to store books and papers he wanted to keep. The hallway of the main house was also piled high with newspapers that Sandburg was going to read but had not yet reached.

Visitors often made the trek up the hill to the house to be welcomed by members of the family. Sandburg was especially pleased when someone purchased one of his Lincoln works and asked for an autograph. His work and friends on the national and international scene left him little time for local affairs. Out of this busy schedule in retirement came the rumor in the community that

Sandburg had little interest in the people of his new home. Actually, Sandburg was very busy in far-distant places like Hollywood, New York, Chicago, and Washington. He was not home sometimes for weeks on end. Sandburg loved children and, as noted, visited schools and entertained them. However, he did not like being used and did not suffer fools grandly.

When Mrs. Sandburg had to come to town, he would occasionally accompany her and sit on a green bench near the Skyland Hotel while waiting. Invariably, Don Barber—the community's leading photographer whose studio was across the street from the Skyland—would photograph him. The *Times-News* would often send a reporter to ask a few questions, but for the most part the press and radio allowed him to be private at home and a celebrity outside of the region. Occasionally he would write a letter to the editor and once had an exchange in print with J. T. Fain, Sr., editor of the paper from 1927 until 1957.

One of the civic clubs asked him to speak, and he accepted only to have preliminaries on the program take up all of his time. So, in classic Sandburg style, he got up, said he was Carl Sandburg, and thanked them for inviting him. Then he sat down. End of speech. Club members were stunned, but the poet gained the eternal gratitude of civic club speakers around the world who had been cut short of time because of introductions, singing of songs, announcements, plans for the next light bulb sale, and endless pranks and jokes.

From 1945 until 1958, Sandburg was out of town much of the time shepherding his many projects and accepting the accolades for nearly a half century of writing and speaking. These were golden years in his life. On his eighty-first birthday, a United Press story from Charlotte called him "aging Carl Sandburg." He called the *Times-News* to complain, thinking that paper had filed the story. There was a sharp exchange between a reporter and Sandburg. When Sandburg realized the paper had nothing to do with the story and word "aging," he mellowed and asked the reporter to visit him. The reporter did, and during one afternoon visit Sandburg said he really was an old newspaperman who made good. He talked about his days on Col. Frank Knox's *Chicago Daily News* and the column that he once wrote for the Galesburg paper. He got a copy of the column and showed the reporter. It was similar to the daily column the reporter wrote for the paper. Sandburg showed his editing ability by telling the reporter that he used too many adjectives. "Strong verbs," Sandburg told the reporter, "use strong verbs." The lesson was well learned. Years afterward, when the reporter had become an editor, the orders on the paper were no adjectives, but strong verbs. Longtime city editor John Dills carried out the edict.

There was a kinship between Sandburg and the paper that few knew about. Sandburg had been a Newspaper Enterprise Association (a Scripps-Howard feature service based in Cleveland) correspondent before, during, and after World War I, and the *Times-News* used NEA stories and features for years. Sandburg once met an army colonel who was visiting Hendersonville, and they talked about West Point. Sandburg told about serving in the Spanish-American War with Company C of the Sixth Illinois in both Cuba and Puerto Rico amid the heat and malaria. He came home a hardened veteran and hero to a proud Swedish family. The officers of Company C honored Sandburg by obtaining for him a congressional appointment to West Point. He told the colonel that he really had wanted to attend the academy; it was something he relished after his war experiences. Sandburg took the train for West Point and the entrance exams only to find he failed both the arithmetic and grammar sections of the test. The deficiencies, he noted, kept him out of the Point. He admitted that for a would-be writer it was a major setback. His war experience gave him an appreciation of patriotism that only veterans can have, and through the years he cherished his membership in the Veterans of Foreign Wars, the veterans' organization that grew out of the Spanish-American War.

Penelope Niven in her book, *Carl Sandburg—A Biography*, noted that in his brief stay at the Point for physical and academic exams in 1899, the veteran of combat as an infantryman in the Spanish-American War marched to formations with two plebes who would become famous as soldiers—Douglas MacArthur and Ulysses S. Grant II. Sandburg would became just as famous, but as a writer, and only after flunking English. The army colonel, the veteran of two tours in Vietnam, never forgot his visit with Sandburg. He, too, went on, becoming a deputy secretary general of the United Nations for Refugees.

Sandburg had an impact on the local Western North Carolina school systems but didn't know it. It came about soon after he had moved to Henderson County. An English teacher at Hendersonville High School, Lucille Kirby Allen, and an English teacher at a county high school, Anne Allen Clement, were taking courses in Asheville toward a masters degree, and one of the projects was to bring in an outside resource program for 140 teachers that would be both educational and entertaining.

Mrs. Allen wrote many years later that the class prevailed upon her to obtain Carl Sandburg, who had created quite a stir in the mountains by moving to Flat Rock. She didn't know that Sandburg received $600 an appearance in those days. She did know that nobody could reach him except through his agent in New York. Edward R. Murrow could reach him, important newsman could reach him, but few others as he worked on his only historical novel, *Remembrance Rock.* He had a full-time secretary and two typists working on the book with him at the time.

"We had one ray of hope," Mrs. Allen wrote. "One in my group shared a common bond—Abraham Lincoln. I knew I couldn't reach him by telephone. We had never met, and my name would simply spell 'impossible,' but I had great faith in the postal service. I wrote and rewrote a letter and mailed it to him." Mrs. Allen's letter made him aware of Lincoln's connection with her hometown of Petersburg, Illinois, and her uncle Harve Rutledge who married her father's only sister, a distant cousin of Anne Rutledge, Lincoln's fiancee, who died of pneumonia before they were to be married. Anne Rutledge, she wrote Sandburg, is buried next to her (Allen's) father, mother, and brother. The letter struck a chord, and Sandburg telephoned Mrs. Allen, agreeing to speak for $2 a head.

Mrs. Allen later wrote that when they went to Connemara to take him to the auditorium, they found, "Sandburg sitting on the porch with his now-familiar green sunshade pulled low to protect his eyes from the midday sun and his guitar, which we asked him to bring, resting across his knees." She said the hour-long program was over all too soon, and Sandburg received ovation after ovation and responded with many encores. It was a triumph for the two Henderson County teachers to have the county's most famous citizen appear.

Alas, it had been a long day, and the teachers were eager to return home. Sandburg spoke: "Now girls, let's not be in a hurry to get home. I've arranged to take the rest of the day off. This is my first opportunity to do a bit of browsing in Asheville, and there are a few things I want to do. I've been too long confined to my desk." Walking slowly toward the car, he continued: "I need to buy a few things. When we get uptown we can park the car, and you girls can help me shop. I want to see the Sondley Library, too. I've passed by but have never been inside. Then, there is a little bookstore somewhere behind the George Vanderbilt Hotel where, I'm told, are to be found some first editions, and I especially want to spend a little time at the Thomas Wolfe home. I'd like to show my appreciation for this lovely trip by taking you girls to a movie, *The Enchanted Forest*, which has been recommended to me, then you are to be my guests for dinner, and you may select the place you'd like to go. Then we can drive home in the cool of the evening."

The agenda left them pretty much speechless, Mrs. Allen later said. "At Wolfe's home, which was the last stop on Sandburg's agenda, he and Tom's brother, Fred, settled into comfortable chairs on the spacious porch. Anne and I found a place apart, and while the two men entered into an hour's rap session about Tom Wolfe and his writings, we planned our strategy for the remainder of the afternoon. We agreed on dinner as soon as we maneuvered this great man toward an eating place. It was too late now to catch a matinee. Our selection was a popular restaurant at Biltmore Plaza, a step in the right direction for us. The only problem was the Plaza didn't open until six, and it was 5:30."

The girls then took Mr. Sandburg across the street to where Anne's two sisters, both nurses, lived in an apartment above a drugstore. Refreshments were served, and the girls asked him to play some songs. The guitar came out, and the concert began. By 7:30, Mrs. Allen said, she and Anne were hungry, but dinner was leisurely and enjoyable. They got home by 10:30 after what Mrs. Allen termed, "a once-in-a-lifetime opportunity." Mrs. Allen and her daughter, Kirby, had Mr. and Mrs. Sandburg to dinner that summer and over the years kept in touch.

Sandburg also helped the Flat Rock Playhouse, located across from Connemara, on several occasions. The late Robroy Farquhar, founder and managing director of the playhouse for nearly forty years, made known to Sandburg on at least one occasion that the playhouse was in the red at the end of the season with bills to pay.

Sandburg came and, to the delight of the playhouse's patrons, presented *An Evening with Carl Sandburg*. During the years there were several *Evenings* with Sandburg at the playhouse until he was unable to perform.

In the 1960s, Sandburg reduced his busy schedule as he aged. Several times the newspaper reported him in the hospital. The paper would report his condition at request of the national press; otherwise, he and the family were given privacy. He passed away at home in the summer of 1967, just a week after the midair collision of a light plane and Piedmont jet airliner near Hendersonville's I-26 and US 64 East intersection that resulted in eighty-two deaths. When Sandburg passed away peacefully at Connemara, Mrs. Sandburg notified CBS and Harry Golden, a family friend in Charlotte who was famous in his own right as an editor and publisher of stories. The local paper received the news late in the morning but remade its front page with eight different one-column photos of Mr. Sandburg with the cutline: The Many Faces of Carl Sandburg. It was the second national story to come out of Hendersonville in one week.

Alden Whitman of the *New York Times*, the reporter who raised obituary writing to an art and whose work still sets the standard for all newspaper people, came to Hendersonville to cover the funeral. He contacted the managing editor of the *Times-News*, who, in turn, arranged for him to meet with Mrs. Sandburg at Connemara. Before dinner and a subsequent visit with Mrs. Sandburg and family at Connemara later in the evening, Whitman obtained a quotation from the Rev. Mack M. Goss, pastor of Hendersonville's First Baptist Church, who had alluded to the poet-author in his Sunday service.

One crisis did come up. Sandburg's family wanted the funeral at Flat Rock's famed old church, St. John-in-the-Wilderness, the Episcopal church that once was Christopher Memminger's private chapel. Sandburg was not an Episcopalian; he was born a Swedish Lutheran but had moved away from that church in his lifetime. Furthermore, a Unitarian minister camping in Pisgah National Forest at the time was to be the officiating minister at the funeral service. The Rev. Walter Roberts, rector of St. John's, presented this conflict with Episcopal policy to the Bishop of Western North Carolina who graciously gave permission for the service of the famous poet in St. John-in-the-Wilderness as long as an Episcopal priest or service was not used. Friends and family of the Sandburgs, as well as Flat Rock neighbors, gathered at the church.

Whitman, who was to write the main story for the *Times*, asked Harry Golden; Ralph McGill, editor of the *Atlanta Constitution* and a friend of Sandburg's; and the managing editor of the *Times-News*, to sit together and sing "John Brown's Body," the alternate words to the "Battle Hymn of the Republic," when the song was to be sung. Somehow the quartet of newspapermen at newspaperman Carl Sandburg's funeral got off on the wrong note and did their best with "John Brown's body lies a-moldering in the grave" while the rest of the audience outsang them with the classic lines of the "Battle Hymn" in the old chapel of the Confederacy in Flat Rock.

Edward Steichen, Sandburg's brother-in-law, provided the perfect touch when he broke off a bough from one of the pines lining the long drive to Connemara and placed it on the casket. Not long after the funeral, the Hendersonville Chamber of Commerce, the *Times-News*, and Congressman Roy A. Taylor contacted Mrs. Sandburg about making Connemara a national historic site honoring Carl Sandburg. She and the family agreed, and the estate passed to the people of the United States under the aegis of the National Park Service. The last home of the "poet of the people" was now in the hands of the people.

NOTE: The Sandburg Historic Site at Flat Rock, operated by the National Park Service, is open to the public on a regular schedule with guided tours and special programs. Parking and shuttle bus are available. Follow the signs at Flat Rock, south of Hendersonville on US 25. The author of this book was a reporter and later managing editor of the Times-News *during Sandburg's later years at Connemara, and knew the poet-author.*

Horace Kephart: Greatest Woodsman of Them All

The Great Smoky Mountains National Park is a national treasure—thanks in part to a shy, mild-mannered, alcoholic librarian who abandoned his wife and six children to recover from a nervous breakdown in what he termed the "back of beyond" in the Smokies in 1904, where he wound up becoming known by many as the "Greatest Woodsman of Them All." Horace Kephart is his name.

Today he is all but forgotten. Hikers on the Appalachian Trail know there is a Mount Kephart in the Smokies but few realize the man for whom the peak is named is one of the founders of the trail. Today's *woodsies* know the name L. L. Bean but probably are not aware that the woodcraft they practice on wilderness camping trips is a direct result of Kephart's knowledge and writing nearly of ninety years ago. The Great Smoky Mountains National Park might be a ravaged timber lode today if Kephart had not taken up the cause to save the wilderness for future generations. Around Bryson City and other environs of the Great Smokies, the tale of Horace Kephart is legend.

It was no accident that Kephart, a St. Louis, Missouri, librarian who had studied at five colleges and universities, found the most remote part of the United States in 1904 for refuge. Abandoning his wife and six children after a breakdown, Kephart consulted maps, books, and literature to find the back of beyond to begin his recovery. The place, he decided, was near Bryson City, North Carolina, in the Great Smoky Mountains, an almost mystical place for the Cherokee Indians who hid amid the lofty peaks and deep coves to thwart their roundup and removal from ancestral lands in the 1830s.

After the Removal of the Cherokee in 1838, called the Trail of Tears, settlers moved into the valleys, coves, hollows, and heights in greater numbers than before. The Smokies were the last frontier, the last wilderness even as other parts of the continent were being conquered by the surge of humanity from east to west in what was called "Manifest Destiny." All the mountains of Western North Carolina and eastern Tennessee were frontier long after the rest of the country, because the terrain made travel difficult. Into the 1920s and '30s, roads were merely widened trails, hugging the steep sides of the mountains. Even in 1945, at the end of World War II, Western North Carolina, from the standpoint of farming, transportation, and culture, was only one decade away from the turn of the century. It was still the land of *make do*. That is exactly what Horace Kephart was looking for.

Kephart claimed his passion for mountains was inherited, as his ancestors were Swiss. They emigrated to the mountains west of the Susquehanna River in Pennsylvania years before the American Revolution. Kephart was born in East Salem, Pennsylvania, in 1862. In 1872, his father, a minister and college professor, moved the family to Jefferson, Iowa, a village on the edge of the prairie wilderness. Writing in the North Carolina Library Bulletin years later, Kephart revealed:

> I had no playmates. My mother taught me to read. When I was seven and could read almost anything, she gave me my first book, dear old Robinson Crusoe. It has been saved through the vicissitudes of a somewhat venturesome life, and lies before me now, coverless and stained with age, but more precious than all the thousands of other books that I afterwards acquired.

Robinson Crusoe was Kephart's handbook for living as a child, one of the keys to his personality in later years. He made a wooden gun, fur cap, hatchet, and knives for use in a child's fantasy world based on the Crusoe stories. He built a cave out of sod, found a derelict rowboat for a ship, and swam to it in imagination, returning with a raft laden with sea chests, barrels of powder, kegs of rum, sails, rope, and other salvage. "Last of all, I found some thirty-six pounds of money, some European coins, some Brazil, some pieces of eight, some gold, and some silver," he wrote of his early days. "And I smiled to myself at the sight of all this money."

There was romance in imagination but not in the real world on the prairie, despite thousands of game birds, animals, and even wild Indians. He would write of the prairie years:

> I never dreamed that such a life and surroundings were romantic. My romance was out there in the sod cave and the crazy old boat among the cottonwoods. The actual savages with whom I was familiar were to me naught but dirty thieves and vagabonds; so I had to invent a good savage for my man Friday. In those days there were thousands of boys far away in the East, many of them living by the seashore, whose highest ambition in life was to go west and fight Indians. I was in the West, and did have to fight now and then with Indians (of my own size), but that was the mere humdrum of daily existence. My fondest dream was to go east and be a sailor boy.

One day he ran away only to be brought up short when the coin he so carefully hoarded for his getaway was refused because it was made of lead, not silver or gold. The experience made him care little for money, a trait that would surface in his move to the mountains.

With an uncle who was president of Western College, Western, Iowa, and a father who was a professor at the same school, Kephart finished high school there and did his freshman year of college at home before finishing up at Lebanon Valley College in Pennsylvania. He received his bachelor of arts degree in 1879, "not without misgivings on the part of the faculty as to my orthodoxy and sundry other qualifications."

Kephart's career path took an unusual turn when he spent the next year in Boston, nominally as a senior at Boston University, as he puts it, "but actually dissecting starfish and so on in the Tech., under Alpheus Hyatt, and enjoying the blessed privilege of studying whatever I pleased in the Boston Public Library."

"The absolute academic freedom of the Library," he said later, "was such a relief to one who had suffered from set curriculums that I resolved to help others find it: I chose librarianship for a career." That is how Kephart became a librarian. Work as a librarian and more study would be Kephart's life for the next twenty years. In 1880, he went to Cornell University, where he supervised cataloguing the library's holdings and took courses in history and political science. He worked for Willard Fiske, Cornell's first librarian. Fiske became Kephart's personal friend and benefactor. When Fiske, who was independently wealthy, went to Italy to assemble world-class collections of Dante and Petrarch, Icelandic history and literature, and the Rhaeto-Romanic language, he hired Kephart to assist in cataloguing and purchasing the materials. This put Kephart in the best libraries in Italy as well as in the Royal Library in Munich. At the same time Kephart attended lectures by Paolo Mantegazza, an eminent anthropologist, at the Institute de studii Superiori. He also took a number of walking trips in the Apennines and Alps. Not bad for a youngster who grew up on the prairie of Iowa.

When he returned to the United States in 1886, he accepted the post of assistant librarian at Yale University in New Haven, Connecticut. It was at Yale that he began his career as a writer. The early work was about library matters. In addition, while at Yale he developed an interest in American frontier history. He had lived it, and now he wanted to know more about it. He also married a girl from Ithaca, Laura White Mack, and they had four daughters and two sons, later all graduates of Cornell. The next move was to St. Louis, where he was librarian of the St. Louis Mercantile Library. This was the oldest library west of the Mississippi. It housed the chief collection of scholarly books in the Mississippi Valley at the time.

Kephart's contribution was to build a special collection of Western Americana; while in the process, he became one of the nation's leading authorities. Western firearms, frontier history, and outdoor life fascinated Kephart. He took time off from his work at the library to seek out materials. It was the time he devoted to the building of this collection that changed Kephart's outlook in life, and yet eventually got him fired by the library's board of directors.

Kephart's home life was also disintegrating. He couldn't stand the confinement or the responsibility of raising a family. Laura wanted him home to help with the children, but he preferred to take camping trips to the Ozark Mountains where he'd devise new camping devices and tents. Because of the trips and a serious drinking problem, the library board put additional pressure on him.

The final event that broke his health was the St. Louis hurricane of 1904. He was caught on a city street during the height of the winds. He grabbed and hung onto a street lamp as people and debris were blown past him. This traumatic experience shattered his already frayed nerves, and he suffered what was known in those days as a nervous breakdown.

After being fired by the library directors, Kephart returned for a while to the home of his parents in Dayton, Ohio, and his wife and six children returned to her home in Ithaca, New York. His biography notes that in Dayton he became preoccupied with starting a literary career and, at the same time, living a wilderness experience. He told friends he wanted "to realize the past in the present—a place to begin again." That is when he first began his search for the back of beyond.

Kephart had noticed earlier, during his search for rare source materials on the western frontier, that the writings were not sufficiently literary, lacking in rich description. Except for Francis Parkman's *Oregon Trail*, Kephart found no intimate and vivid account of the hunters and trappers who'd won the West. He wanted to continue this idea of putting flesh on the dry bones of history. It was while he worked at this writing that the catastrophe of the hurricane had struck, not only at the heart of St. Louis but at Kephart's already buffeted heart. He had to seek a quiet place in which to restart his life and regain his inner composure, so he began consulting maps in an effort to find the most remote part of the country.

He finally pinpointed Swain County, North Carolina, as the place, took a train to Asheville, and then to Dillsboro, where he found a place to stay on Dick's Creek before finding his back of beyond. Horace Kephart's back of beyond was a small cabin at the abandoned Adams copper mine on the Little Fork of the Sugar Fork of Hazel Creek, high in the Smokies near Bryson City. The Adams mine was a mile or two from a place called Medlin, consisting of four houses and Granville Calhoun's store and post office. It was

Calhoun who fetched the weak and ailing Kephart from the train at the Ritter station, now buried under the waters of Lake Fontana. Calhoun, the squire of Hazel Creek, answered a plea from Dr. C. D. W. Colby of Asheville, a friend of Kephart's. It was an exile of sorts, one that Kephart would come to relish, one that would give him back his health. With health came the desire to work again. "To one coming from cities, it was a strange environment, almost as though one had been carried back, asleep, upon the wings of time, and had awakened in the eighteenth century, to meet Daniel Boone in flesh and blood," he wrote.

For three years he remained in exile in the virgin forest of the Great Smokies. As one woman said, he was more Indian than the Cherokees who lived in Swain and Graham counties. Kephart said he never felt lonesome in the day, but as the black nights closed in, the owls began to call the *blue devils* out of the woods; sometimes Kephart's beloved seclusion could turn to isolation, calling forth the strange thoughts all people get when alone too much. To strike a balance, he needed something to take his mind off his solitude in the remote forest. That is when he wrote his first book, *Camping and Woodcraft*, a classic in the field. Over the years he expanded it until the final editions had over nine hundred pages.

While woodcraft and camping interested him, Kephart also became intrigued with the people who populated his beloved back of beyond. These were real people who lived real lives. He wrote in the *North Carolina Literary Bulletin*:

> I became more absorbed in study of my human associates in the backwoods. They were unlike any people I had ever met elsewhere. They were like figures taken from the old frontier histories and legends that I had been so fond of, only they were living flesh and blood instead of mere characters in books. I seemed to be actually living among the pioneer farmers and herdsmen and hunters, the trappers and traders, the teachers and preachers, the outlaws and the Indians of a hundred and fifty years ago. They interested me more than the ultracivilized folk of cities.

Kephart found what many before him and generations after understood—the southern highlands of the Blue Ridge and Great Smokies are seductive. Its people are among the finest in the world.

Kephart, adrift in the rat race of his time, found peace in the Smokies. He hunted bear with wily mountain men; fished for brook trout in streams; bandaged the hurt and injured as a quasi doctor; listened to the stories of the mountain men before the hearth and campfire; treated his newfound friends as equals; and he knew how to survive in the wilderness of the Smokies better than most. After three years Kephart returned to civilization in Bryson City—still a remote place—and lived at the town's leading hotel, the Cooper House, where he became fast friends with "Uncle" Billy Cooper, owner of the hotel. Other friends included I. K. Stems, whose family ran a sawmill; Kelly "Doc" Bennett, the local druggist; Will Wiggins, a timber cruiser; and George Masa, the famous Smokies photographer from Asheville.

Kephart camped in the hinterlands during summer, often at the old Bryson Place, eight miles from the present Deep Creek Campground. Around Bryson City, the county seat of Swain County, Kephart was somewhat of a local attraction because of his books on camping. The Cooper House was often called Kephart Tavern by local residents. Those who knew him said he was a well-mannered, quiet person who actually sought to avoid the limelight. His periodic drinking bouts were well known, but when they came he remained in his room and caused no problems.

He was so fascinated with the southern highlanders that he began travels into Tennessee, Kentucky, and Georgia to see if the people there were similar to those in Western North Carolina. To his amazement, they were. He became convinced they were one people. That is when he began work on his classic, *Our Southern Highlanders*, the book that put Horace Kephart on the literary map.

When published in 1913, the book brought out critics who said the mountaineers were not as Kephart portrayed them. Alas, the critics failed to note that Kephart wrote about the mountain people in the coves, hollows, and heights rather than the farmers on the bottom lands and towns. There were three kinds of people back then: the townspeople, who often were educated and sophisticated; the wealthy bottomland farmers; and the people along the ridges and in the coves. Kephart answered his critics by saying he lived with the people and the critics had not, and the people were still his friends many years later. They would not have been his friends had he not told the truth.

Even today the book is a classic. Kephart agreed with the critics that the book was fragmented and sketchy. He said that was the way his life was, and the book was partly autobiographical. He left out some: his drinking, his money, his family life, and any romances. As he noted, the best stories are those that are never told. Of the money, he said his first fortune was imaginary, and the second was counterfeit. What need of money only to purchase fishing rods, books, and guns? The people of the "back of beyond" were those who *made do*. Kephart learned from them.

His writing continued. In addition to *Our Southern Highlanders* and *Camping and Woodcraft*, he wrote *Camp Cookery* and *Sporting Firearms*, two fields in which he was expert; *Camping and Camper Manual*; and edited a series of volumes of adventure and exploration called *Outdoor Adventures Library*. He worked on a novel, *Smoky Mountain Magic*, but never published it.

On one of his summer camping trips in 1906 to a herder's hut six miles east of Thunderhead Mountain in the Smokies, Kephart heard the staccato huffing of a Little River Railroad Shay engine where before the silence had been deafening. It was on the Tennessee side of the divide, where in 1901, Col. E. B. Townsend of Pennsylvania had purchased eighty-six thousand acres in the Little River section of the Smokies. The colonel was getting forty thousand board feet per acre from Tuckaleechee Cove to Clingmans Dome. The engine Kephart heard was part of the trackage that ran up the coves, along Little River to Elkmont in one direction, Cades Cove in the other, and west from the Little River wye to the village of Townsend, where the band mill was located. Today the Little River Railroad roadbed is the automobile road from Sugarlands to Cades Cove and Townsend.

Sounds of the steam engine in the Smokies upset Kephart. All that summer, as he hiked from place to place, tending to the needs of the people who inhabited the coves and heights, Kephart heard the shunting of the engines, the puffing of Clyde steam log loaders, and the whine of saws amid the crashing of the giants of the forest. Sound carries in the mountains, and Kephart realized he was hearing the death knell of the Smokies. And it was happening quite rapidly.

Soon after the turn of the century, after all of the forests of Maine, upstate New York, Michigan, Ohio, Indiana, and Illinois had been devastated by the loggers, lumber companies began moving into West Virginia and Kentucky. It was while the timber men were working the mountains in these two states that word reached their headquarters that the once inaccessible Smokies could be logged if gear-driven Shay and Climax railroad engines were used instead of oxen and horses and the new Clyde log loader and overhead skidder set up to move logs rather than snaking them out of the forest.

Until that time the small, local sawmills took a few trees at a time from landowners who depended on the hard cash the trees brought. Given the extent of logging in the Smokies under that arrangement, the trees would last forever. Agents of the lumber companies moved rapidly to buy the land from owners or acquire the timber rights. In some cases, it was a race to see who could gain the most land. As noted, Colonel Townsend arrived in 1901 on the Tennessee side. Ritter Lumber Company began acquiring land from the owners in the Hazel Creek section in 1903, the year before Kephart arrived, but the parcels were few. By 1909, Ritter had a band mill at Proctor that produced seventy thousand board feet of lumber a day. A firm from Glasgow, Scotland, Scottish Carolina Timber and Land, built a large mill at Newport at the northern end of the Smokies; Parsons Pulp and Lumber built a mill at Ravensfork on the Oconaluftee River; and Champion, a paper mill that operates even today at Canton, North Carolina, acquired its first land near Canton in 1905. Within a few years Champion, an Ohio firm, had acquired ninety-two thousand acres in the heart of the Smokies.

Kephart knew loggers had begun chewing into the great virgin forest known as the Smokies but not to what extent. He also knew that fire followed the loggers and a report made in 1901 predicted dire consequences if the rate of logging was to continue. Kephart asked himself over and over, "why?" He considered rape of the land, land that has provided life and liberty to the people of the Appalachians, a cruel fate. He saw Mount Mitchell in the Black Mountains of the Blue Ridge, highest peak east of the Rockies, nearly destroyed. Now it was his beloved Smokies' turn. Kephart, an author, began to write.

Over and over in publications, he asked, "why?" Why should this virgin wilderness, this last hoard of the resources of nature in the eastern half of the land, this birthplace of rivers, this sanctuary for the vanishing wildlife of America, be doomed by greed to extinction? Little is left of the primitive, little of the proud forest which those first Americans subdued, little of untainted wilderness. Why should the little be wiped away? Why should these Smoky Mountains, with their potent, alluring, inescapable charm—the power that dragged the Cherokee back through hunger and danger and despair, to his high, quiet hills—be surrendered to the smoke-stack and the sawdust heap and the charring of conflagrations? The mountains belonged to America. Let them be preserved for the Americans of every generation.

Kephart was preaching the need for a Great Smoky Mountains National Park. Of course, the timber men were uneasy with this writer who proposed a park amid their valued timberlands. Their motto was: get in and out of the forest with the highest possible yields and profits and don't worry about fire, flood, or future generations. Because Kephart was a respected writer, he got attention. Slowly the message filtered out. More and more public officials picked up the idea, both in Tennessee and North Carolina. It wasn't just trees that garnered their attention; they also the realized that the Smokies are the watershed for much of the southern United States. Water, precious water, came from the mountains. To keep the flow untainted, the watershed needed preservation. To keep the flow even, there needed to be trees. The logic cut through the greed of the free enterprisers of the day, the lumbermen. Even the *Asheville Citizen*, a paper whose readers included the people dependent on lumber, championed the cause, much to the dismay of Champion Paper Company and other loggers.

Various commissions were formed, and after years of wrangling, political trading, outright transfer of funds from one account to another, and a massive $5 million gift from John D. Rockefeller, Jr., deeds for the Great Smoky Mountains National Park were transferred in 1934 by Tennessee, North Carolina, and private interests to the United States government. The lumber companies, despite attempts by U.S. House Speaker "Uncle" Joe Cannon to derail the park idea, were finally defeated. President Franklin D. Roosevelt, who backed the idea and even siphoned funds from the Civilian Conservation Corps to help pay for some of the land, was elated. He dedicated the park in 1940 in a ceremony at Newfound Gap.

Horace Kephart wasn't there. He died in an automobile accident on April 2, 1931, near Ela, between Bryson City and Cherokee, while on a taxi trip from Bryson City to his bootlegger. Killed in the accident along with Kephart was his close friend and author, Fiswoode Tarleton, a resident of Decatur, Georgia. Tarleton was visiting Kephart because his health was poor, and Kephart had done so well in the mountains with his recovery. The taxi driver, R. R. Brown, was injured. Funeral services were held for both men at the Bryson City Cemetery, and Kephart was buried in the lot of Jack Coburn, overlooking the town of Bryson City and the mountains. Mrs. Kephart and his two sons attended the funeral. In 1936, an eight-ton boulder from the Chasteen-Reagan place above Smokemont was moved by the local Civilian Conservation Corps unit and placed over the grave.

Soon after Kephart was killed, members of the Appalachian Trail Conference eulogized him. Paul Fink, an attorney from Jonesboro, Tennessee, and one of Kephart's close friends, summed it best, as carried in the organization's bulletin, when he said,

> The greatest woodsman of them all has tramped his last trail, climbed his last mountain and has made his last camp. As his friends the Cherokee would phrase it, Horace Kephart has followed the "Western Trail to the Darkening Land." Kephart had long cherished the idea of a national park in the Smokies. When public sentiment finally crystallized into action, he immediately laid aside other matters and enthusiastically threw all his efforts into the work. Letters, magazine and newspaper articles, personal influence, all the forces he had at his disposal, were put behind the movement, and we know that his personality, and reputation, played a large part toward arousing the outside, as well as local sentiment, that has carried on the project until now its final consummation is just around the corner. Such a pity that he could not have lived to see his dream come true.

Kephart's loss was felt keenly, not only by the Appalachian Trail Conference, but also by those who depended upon him to lead the fight for the national park. Just a short time before his death, the government named a peak in the Smokies, Mount Kephart, in honor of the woodsman. His idealistic dream of a Great Smoky

Mountains National Park came into being. Many were involved in bringing the park to reality, but the man who used the written and spoken word so effectively to sell the park to the public, thus forcing public officials to take notice, never got to attend the ceremony transferring the deeds, or the dedication. Yet, as the park became reality, his friends said it was not his works but "his personality, the man himself" that endeared him to all he met.

Fink said he was a "real gentleman in all things, quiet and unassuming, with an aversion for public appearance, much preferring to forgather with a few chosen friends, where without effort he assumed his natural place as center of the circle. Always true to his convictions, willing to fight to the last ditch for that which his high ideals told him was right, he was ever charitable toward those on the opposing side of the question, never stooping to personalities, even though the ammunition was plentiful at his hand and the provocation great." And as his friends had often noted, money didn't count with Kephart. Fink echoed their sentiments, saying, "When funds were plentiful with him he drew far greater joy in relieving the needs of some friend than in purchasing comforts and luxuries for himself. It was one of his most predominant characteristics. He fought their battles, shared their sorrows, relieved their distresses to the limit of his ability, and rejoiced more in their achievements than he did in his own. Nothing in his power was too great for him to do for them and no more appropriate epitaph for him could be written than the words of I. K. Sterns, his closest companion, 'Kep's last act, like most of his acts, was doing a favor for a friend.'"

Horace Kephart helped bring about the Great Smoky Mountains National Park to help his friends, the people of the Smokies, and then, with the task complete except for some details, followed his beloved Cherokee "Western Trail to the Darkening Land" on the road near Ela while doing a favor for a friend. That's why in the hinterlands, Horace Kephart is a legend.

NOTE: Horace Kephart's papers are at Western Carolina University. Hiking trails to the Bryson Place start at Deep Creek Campground. Hazel Creek is still a favorite of trout fishermen. It may be reached by boat. Lake Fontana covers Ritter and other towns Kephart knew.

Index

David Hooks Photography

Mead Parce was a newspaper editor with a lifelong interest in history and the mountain people of the Southern Appalachians. A graduate of Utica College of Syracuse University, he lived in such diverse places as Texas, Utah, Florida, Central New York, New England, and Hawaii before settling in Hendersonville, North Carolina. There he was the editor of the community's daily newspaper, the Times-News, for a number of years. In addition to editing the paper, he wrote six columns a week, many involving local history.